SpringerBriefs in Business

SpringerBriefs present concise summaries of cutting-edge research and practical applications across a wide spectrum of fields. Featuring compact volumes of 50 to 125 pages, the series covers a range of content from professional to academic. Typical topics might include:

- A timely report of state-of-the art analytical techniques
- A bridge between new research results, as published in journal articles, and a contextual literature review
- A snapshot of a hot or emerging topic
- An in-depth case study or clinical example
- A presentation of core concepts that students must understand in order to make independent contributions

SpringerBriefs in Business showcase emerging theory, empirical research, and practical application in management, finance, entrepreneurship, marketing, operations research, and related fields, from a global author community.

Briefs are characterized by fast, global electronic dissemination, standard publishing contracts, standardized manuscript preparation and formatting guidelines, and expedited production schedules.

More information about this series at http://www.springer.com/series/8860

Mariella Pinna

Sustainable Entrepreneurship

A Systematic Review of Academic Research

Springer

Mariella Pinna
Department of Economics and Business
University of Sassari
Sassari, Italy

ISSN 2191-5482 ISSN 2191-5490 (electronic)
SpringerBriefs in Business
ISBN 978-3-030-57817-6 ISBN 978-3-030-57818-3 (eBook)
https://doi.org/10.1007/978-3-030-57818-3

This Springer imprint is published by the registered company Springer Nature Switzerland AG.
The registered company address is: Gewerbestrasse 11, 6330 Cham, Switzerland

To my parents Rita and Gérard,
for their constant support.

To Achille,
for teaching me the value of waiting.

To Andrea,
for pushing me to overcome my limits and
being by my side.

Acknowledgments

This work is part of the research project "Understanding Positive and Negative drivers of Sustainable Entrepreneurship intentions" funded by the Sardinian Government, R.L. 7/2007 "*Young Researchers Mobility Program*." This research was also supported by the Italian Ministry of Education (MIUR): "*Dipartimenti di Eccellenza Program* (2018–2022)"—Department of Economics and Business—University of Sassari.

I wish to express my gratitude to Professor Kai Hockerts for his supervision during my stay at Copenhagen Business School (DK). Thank you for sharing your knowledge with me and for precious suggestions during the collection and analysis of the data.

Very special thanks are due to Professor Ludovico Marinò and Professor Katia Corsi for their continuous support and encouragement during my career.

Special thanks are also due to the reviewers for their insightful comments and helpful suggestions.

Finally, I would like to thank the administrative staff of the Department of Economics and Business of the University of Sassari for their helpful support in the preparation of the manuscript.

Contents

Chapter 1
Introduction

Sustainable Entrepreneurship has been gaining momentum in international academic debates (e.g., Muñoz, Janssen, Nicolopoulou, & Hockerts, 2018). Since the concept of sustainable entrepreneurship first appeared in academic research,[1] a sharp increase in the number of workshops and conference sessions taking place throughout the world, as well as publications and special issues in top journals,[2] have been noted (Muñoz & Cohen, 2018).

Sustainable entrepreneurship is a new field of research (Shepherd & Patzelt, 2011) that stems from the entrepreneurship literature, from which it borrows theoretical underpinnings and methodological approaches, but then it expands into sustainability science as its "natural fellow field" (Muñoz & Cohen, 2017, p. 1). Such cross-pollination has involved a step-by-step process. Originally, the discussion on sustainable development focused on whether and how the inclusion of social and environmental concerns into corporate goals would benefit the company (Jermier, Forbes, Benn, & Orsato, 2006). More recently, as traditional entrepreneurship has failed to answer the triple challenges of sustainability (i.e., people, planet, profit) (Munoz & Dimov, 2015), the debate has shifted to the emerging role of entrepreneurs as facilitators of sustainable development (York & Venkataraman, 2010).

Within this body of knowledge, sustainable entrepreneurship has been referred to as the entrepreneurial process of exploiting opportunities while simultaneously seeking social, environmental, and economic interests (Shepherd & Patzelt, 2011). Such multi-purpose nature of sustainable entrepreneurship has allowed researchers to frame it within the realm of *hybrid businesses* (Doherty, Haugh, & Lyon, 2014). Indeed, hybrid ventures are able to reconcile the pursuit of financial performance and

---

[1]According to our search, the first article dates back to 2002; namely, Keijzers (2002). The transition to the sustainable enterprise. *Journal of Cleaner Production*, 10 (4), 349–359.

[2]e.g., Journal of Business Venturing, 2010; International Journal of Entrepreneurial Behavior and Research, 2018; International Journal of Entrepreneurial Venturing, 2018.

M. Pinna, *Sustainable Entrepreneurship*, SpringerBriefs in Business,
https://doi.org/10.1007/978-3-030-57818-3_1

the fulfilment of social and environmental objectives. To put it simply, the exploitation of business opportunities, which is the core characteristic of entrepreneurship, goes hand-in-hand with the goal of creating value that persists over time, with an overall concern for the well-being of future generations (Hockerts & Wüstenhagen, 2010). To this extent, sustainable entrepreneurship differs from other, although often wrongly associated, typologies of *purpose-driven entrepreneurship* (Stubbs, 2017), such as social (Bacq & Janssen, 2011) and environmental (Linnanen, 2002) entrepreneurship. Two main differences occur in terms of framing the boundaries of the one and the other. First, both social and environmental entrepreneurship, respectively and alternately, have privileged the creation of value for society or for the environment. More simply, social and environmental entrepreneurship represent single frames of the whole sustainability picture (Tilley & Parrish, 2006). Second, sustainable businesses must be financially sustainable to survive (Hall, Daneke, & Lenox, 2010); therefore, any organization relying on public or private funding does not ultimately respond to the triple challenges of sustainability (Shepherd & Patzelt, 2011). Table 1.1 briefly outlines the most popular definitions of sustainable entrepreneurship in chronological order.

The aim of this book is to present a comprehensive assessment of the field of sustainable entrepreneurship, starting with a pool of over 400 published studies and filtering this collection to more relevant and fitting works, in accordance to the review approach adopted. A quantitative (i.e., bibliometric analysis) and qualitative assessment of the scientific research on sustainable development has been completed, and five major clusters of research have been inspected. Such clusters allow us to identify, at a glance, and classify the structure of the research in the field of sustainable entrepreneurship. A qualitative assessment of the clusters is performed by looking at the content of the papers included in each cluster. Based on the aforementioned results, critical insights on the current state of sustainable entrepreneurship research are offered and potential directions for future research are suggested.

Perhaps more importantly, this study offers several contributions to the understanding of sustainable entrepreneurship phenomena and the future of the research field for theory and practice. To the author's best knowledge, this is the first study that provides a complete view of sustainable entrepreneurship on the basis of a review that relies on both objective and subjective approaches. In particular, this is the first review that uses bibliographic coupling as a bibliometric methodology, thus looking at the frontiers of research, rather than capturing the traditional roots of the field (i.e., for a co-citation analysis review, see Terán-Yépez et al., 2020). Second, this volume provides a broad and multifaceted assessment of the progress of the discipline over the past two decades by focusing on the key themes of extant research as well as highlighting promising research gaps to investigate in future studies.

The remainder of the volume is structured as follows: Chap. 2 provides a brief summary of how the field has been reviewed in the past. Chapter 3 outlines the review routine adopted in the volume (i.e., the search, screening, and refinement phases) and the methodology used to analyze the data (i.e., bibliometric and content analyses). Chapter 4 delves into the bibliometric results, both looking at bibliometric

Table 1.1 Summary of current definitions of sustainable entrepreneurship

Authors	Year	Definition
Crals and Vereeck	2004	Sustainable Entrepreneurship is the continuing commitment by businesses to behave ethically and contribute to economic development while improving the quality of life of the workforce, their families, local communities, the society, and the world at large, as well as future generations
Cohen and Winn	2007	Sustainable entrepreneurship is the examination of how opportunities to bring into existence future goods and services are discovered, created, and exploited, by whom and with what economic, psychological, social, and environmental consequences
Dean and McMullen	2007	Sustainable entrepreneurship is the process of discovering, evaluating, and exploiting economic opportunities that are present in market failures which detract from sustainability, including those that are environmentally relevant
Katsikis and Kyrgidou	2007	Sustainable entrepreneurship is the teleological process aiming at the achievement of sustainable development by discovering, evaluating, and exploiting opportunities and creating value that produces economic prosperity, social cohesion, and environmental protection
Parrish and Foxon	2009	Sustainability-driven entrepreneurship describes those entrepreneurial activities in which the central guiding purpose is to make a substantial contribution to sustainable development. More specifically, sustainability entrepreneurs design ventures with the primary intention of contributing to improved environmental quality and social well-being in ways that are mutually supportive
Tilley and Young	2009	A sustainability entrepreneur is an individual who holistically integrates the goals of economic, social, and environmental entrepreneurship into an organization that is sustainable in its goal and sustainable in its form of wealth generation
O'Neill et al.	2009	Sustainability entrepreneurship is a process of venture creation that links the activities of entrepreneurs to the emergence of value-creating enterprises that contribute to the sustainable development of the social–ecological system
Hockerts and Wüstenhagen	2010	Sustainable entrepreneurship is the discovery and exploitation of economic opportunities through the generation of market disequilibria that initiate the transformation of a sector towards an environmentally and socially more sustainable state
Pacheco et al.	2010	Sustainable entrepreneurship is the discovery, creation, evaluation, and exploitation of opportunities to create future goods and services consistent with sustainable development goals
Kuckertz and Wagner	2010	Sustainable development-oriented entrepreneurs are those individuals with entrepreneurial intentions who aim to manage a triple bottom line
Patzel and Shepherd	2010	Sustainable entrepreneurship is the discovery, creation, and exploitation of opportunities to create future goods and services that sustain the natural and/or communal environment and provide development gain for others
Shepherd and Patzel	2011	Sustainable entrepreneurship is focused on the preservation of nature, life support, and community in the pursuit of perceived

(continued)

Table 1.1 (continued)

Authors	Year	Definition
		opportunities to bring into existence future products, processes, and services for gain, where gain is broadly construed to include economic and non-economic gains to individuals, the economy, and society
Schaltegger and Wagner	2011	Sustainable entrepreneurship can be described as an innovative, market-oriented, and personality-driven form of creating economic and societal value by means of breakthrough environmentally or socially beneficial market or institutional innovations
Lans et al.	2014	Sustainable entrepreneurship is a way of generating competitive advantages by identifying sustainability as new business opportunities, resulting in new and sustainable products, methods of production, or ways of organizing business processes in a sustainable way.
Belz and Binder	2017	Sustainable entrepreneurship is the recognition, development, and exploitation of opportunities by individuals to bring into existence future goods and services with economic, social, and ecological gains
Urbaniec	2018	Sustainable entrepreneurship comprises the types of business development practices that provide new opportunities for innovative corporate activities at the nexus of ecological and social issues

Source: Adapted from Muñoz and Cohen (2018), Terán-Yépez, Marín-Carrillo, del Pilar Casado-Belmonte, and de las Mercedes Capobianco-Uriarte (2020)

performance indicators (i.e., the publication trend and the most important actors, such as authors, journals, and institutions) and scientific mapping (i.e., Network Analysis). Chapter 5 focuses on qualitative content analysis with the aim of systematizing the realm of sustainable entrepreneurship research. Chapter 6 offers critical insights into the bibliometric and content analyses by discussing what has been achieved and what still needs to be done in sustainable entrepreneurship research. Managerial implications of the study and future lines of research are also discussed. Finally, Chap. 7 summarizes the main findings of the volume, discusses the limitations of the review approach adopted, and suggests possible new paths of investigation for scholars.

References

Bacq, S., & Janssen, F. (2011). The Multiple Faces of Social Entrepreneurship: A Review of Definitional Issues Based on Geographical and Thematic Criteria. *Entrepreneurship & Regional Development, 23*(5–6), 373–403. https://doi.org/10.1080/08985626.2011.577242

Doherty, B., Haugh, H., & Lyon, F. (2014). Social Enterprises as Hybrid Organizations: A Review and Research Agenda. *International Journal of Management Reviews, 16*(4), 417–436. https://doi.org/10.1111/ijmr.12028

Hall, J. K., Daneke, G. A., & Lenox, M. J. (2010). Sustainable Development and Entrepreneurship: Past Contributions and Future Directions. *Journal of Business Venturing, 25*(5), 439–448. https://doi.org/10.1016/j.jbusvent.2010.01.002

Hockerts, K., & Wüstenhagen, R. (2010). Greening Goliaths Versus Emerging Davids—Theorizing About the Role of Incumbents and New Entrants in Sustainable Entrepreneurship. *Journal of Business Venturing, 25*(5), 481–492. https://doi.org/10.1016/j.jbusvent.2009.07.005

Jermier, J. M., Forbes, L. C., Benn, S., & Orsato, R. J. (2006). The New Corporate Environmentalism and Green Politics. In *The SAGE Handbook of Organization Studies* (pp. 618–650). Thousand Oaks, CA: SAGE Publications Ltd. https://doi.org/10.4135/9781848608030.n22.

Linnanen, L. (2002). An Insider's Experiences with Environmental Entrepreneurship. *Greener Management International, 2002*(38), 71–80. https://doi.org/10.9774/GLEAF.3062.2002.su.00008

Muñoz, P., & Cohen, B. (2017). Towards a Social-Ecological Understanding of Sustainable Venturing. *Journal of Business Venturing Insights, 7*, 1–8. Scopus. https://doi.org/10.1016/j.jbvi.2016.12.001

Muñoz, P., & Cohen, B. (2018). Sustainable Entrepreneurship Research: Taking Stock and looking ahead. *Business Strategy and the Environment, 27*(3), 300–322. Scopus. https://doi.org/10.1002/bse.2000

Munoz, P., & Dimov, D. (2015). The Call of the Whole in Understanding the Development of Sustainable Ventures. *Journal of Business Venturing, 30*(4), 632–654. https://doi.org/10.1016/j.jbusvent.2014.07.012

Muñoz, P., Janssen, F., Nicolopoulou, K., & Hockerts, K. (2018). Advancing Sustainable Entrepreneurship Through Substantive Research. *International Journal of Entrepreneurial Behavior & Research, 24*(2), 322–332. https://doi.org/10.1108/IJEBR-03-2018-427

Shepherd, D. A., & Patzelt, H. (2011). The New Field of Sustainable Entrepreneurship: Studying Entrepreneurial Action Linking «What Is to Be Sustained» With «What Is to Be Developed». *Entrepreneurship: Theory and Practice, 35*(1), 137–163. Scopus. https://doi.org/10.1111/j.1540-6520.2010.00426.x

Stubbs, W. (2017). Sustainable Entrepreneurship and B Corps. *Business Strategy and the Environment, 26*(3), 331–344. Scopus. https://doi.org/10.1002/bse.1920

Terán-Yépez, E., Marín-Carrillo, G. M., del Pilar Casado-Belmonte, M., & de las Mercedes Capobianco-Uriarte, M. (2020). Sustainable Entrepreneurship: Review of Its Evolution and New Trends. *Journal of Cleaner Production, 252*, 119742. https://doi.org/10.1016/j.jclepro.2019.119742

Tilley, F., & Parrish, B. D. (2006). From Poles to Wholes: Facilitating an Integrated Approach to Sustainable Entrepreneurship. *World Review of Entrepreneurship, Management and Sustainable Development, 2*(4), 281–294. Scopus. https://doi.org/10.1504/WREMSD.2006.010214

York, J. G., & Venkataraman, S. (2010). The Entrepreneur–Environment Nexus: Uncertainty, Innovation, and Allocation. *Journal of Business Venturing, 25*(5), 449–463. https://doi.org/10.1016/j.jbusvent.2009.07.007

Chapter 2
Sustainable Entrepreneurship: Framing the Boundaries of Current Knowledge

The interest of academics towards sustainable entrepreneurship has rapidly increased over the last two decades. The history of sustainable entrepreneurship research dates back to Keijzers's seminal paper in 2002. Since then, researchers have been challenged to understand whether and how entrepreneurship, as a panacea for transitioning towards a more sustainable society, actually unfolds (Hall, Daneke, & Lenox, 2010). Despite being in its infancy, several reviews on sustainable entrepreneurship have been published over the past few years.

The majority of these reviews are general and comprehensively cover the entire field of sustainable entrepreneurship (e.g., Terán-Yépez, Marín-Carrillo, del Pilar Casado-Belmonte, & de las Mercedes Capobianco-Uriarte, 2020), while others have focused on specific aspects, such as looking at the description and definition of the concept of sustainable entrepreneurship (Aghelie, Sorooshian, & Azizan, 2016), providing evidence on particular features of sustainable entrepreneurship (Muñoz & Cohen, 2018), or shedding light on the connections between entrepreneurship and sustainable development (Fellnhofer, Kraus, & Bouncken, 2014). For instance, Levinsohn (2013) was the first scholar to critically review papers pertaining the field of sustainable entrepreneurship, looking at 42 papers which appeared in the Web of Science between 1999 and 2010. Building on the *Critical Management Study* perspective, the author delved into the main themes addressed in sustainable entrepreneurship articles and the extent to which these papers actually reflected the triple nature of the sustainable development concept. According to the author, ten primary themes emerged from the literature. Specifically, the first theme, *Green emphasis*, argues for the importance of sustainable entrepreneurship in relation to the environment (e.g., Schaltegger & Wagner, 2011). *The impact of the individual* assesses how values, identities, and cognition affect the behavior of the entrepreneur in relation to sustainability (e.g., Schlange, 2006). The theme *Sustainable entrepreneurship as an expansion of entrepreneurship* deals with the ability of entrepreneurship to create new firms and economic value, and to act as a *trait d'union* between businesses and society, thus promoting institutional change (e.g., Gibbs, 2006).

M. Pinna, *Sustainable Entrepreneurship*, SpringerBriefs in Business,
https://doi.org/10.1007/978-3-030-57818-3_2

Further, the theme *Sustainable entrepreneurship as a business opportunity* uncovers the existence of market opportunities and how sustainable entrepreneurs might discover and exploit them (e.g., Dean & McMullen, 2007). Moreover, according to the category *Sustainable entrepreneurship as embedded*, individuals and their contexts jointly affect the development of sustainable entrepreneurship (e.g., Hockerts & Wüstenhagen, 2010). One trendy topic in the sustainable entrepreneurship literature is *Sustainable entrepreneurship as innovation*, which has been explained in terms of (1) the degree of innovation that takes places (incremental vs. radical), (2) the focus of innovation (i.e., social, process, or product), and (3) the nature of innovation, being tangible or intangible (e.g., Abrahamsson, 2003). Additional themes deal with *the engagement of SMEs in sustainable entrepreneurship and the factors that affect them* (e.g., Moore & Manring, 2009) and *the discussion of sustainable development*, which sheds light on the contested nature of the concept, in order to understand how it connects to entrepreneurship (e.g., Tilley & Parrish, 2006). More specifically, according to Levinsohn (2013) sustainable entrepreneurship has been alternatively conceived by scholars as *double bottom line* (i.e., a combination of two areas of sustainability) (e.g., Hart & Christensen, 2002) or as *triple bottom line* (i.e., a combination of three areas of sustainability) (e.g., Parrish, 2010).

A year later, Fellnhofer et al. (2014) systematically reviewed the research field of sustainable entrepreneurship and identified three main themes in the literature. The first theme—namely, *"from social and environmental entrepreneurship to sustainable entrepreneurial innovation"*—sheds light on the importance of innovation as a main driver of sustainable entrepreneurship (i.e., eco-innovation or social innovation) (e.g., Hockerts & Wüstenhagen, 2010; Schaltegger & Wagner, 2011). Further, the second topic—*"from an economic point of view to corporate sustainability"*—groups together papers that investigate sustainable entrepreneurship within the subset of corporate social responsibility, basically looking at how firms can reduce their environmental impacts and how sustainable development actually affects their competitive advantage (e.g., Atiq & Karatas-Ozkan, 2013). Finally, "*sustainability as an integral part of entrepreneurship*" is the common topic in articles that understand sustainable entrepreneurship as a new solution that blends economic, social, and environmental aims to overcome market disequilibria/failures (e.g., Cohen & Winn, 2007).

In 2016, Aghelie et al. (2016) conducted a literature review on 43 articles focusing on the broad description and definition of the concept of sustainable entrepreneurship. However, the authors did not explain neither the database and the key terms used, nor the methodological approach adopted.

In the following year, two review studies were conducted (Gast, Gundolf, & Cesinger, 2017; Greco & de Jong, 2017). In their contribution, Greco and de Jong (2017) illustrated the most common definitions of sustainable entrepreneurship, the overarching themes, and the applied methods in the field. Recurring themes in sustainable entrepreneurship are related to (1) new venture creation, (2) entrepreneurial drivers, and (3) performance and institutions. New venture creation is seen as the result of the connection of three elements: individuals, environment, and process.

Examples of these elements are business model innovation (e.g., Bocken, 2015), the entrepreneur's traits (e.g., Lans, Blok, & Wesselink, 2014), the financing means (e.g., Miller & Wesley, 2010), the policy interactions (e.g., Pinkse & Groot, 2015), and the institutional influence (e.g., Spence, Ben Boubaker Gherib, & Biwolé, 2011). Finally, according to the authors, different methods are adopted in the field of sustainable entrepreneurship, ranging from quantitative to qualitative and mixed research methodologies. For instance, survey-based studies rely on international (e.g., the Global Entrepreneurship Monitor survey), national, or regional databases to retrieve data on enterprises, while mixed methods usually combine semi-structured case studies with interviews or surveys.

On the other hand, Gast et al. (2017) applied a systematic evidence-informed literature review on a sample of 114 articles published between 1996 and 2015. Their main contribution was the description of a novel framework based on the identification of six clusters and ten sub-themes reflecting the core principles of the classic entrepreneurship process. More specifically, the first cluster focuses on the internal (e.g., individual characteristics) and external (e.g., market imperfections, market failures) factors that drive individuals towards sustainable entrepreneurship (e.g., Cohen & Winn, 2007; Kirkwood & Walton, 2010). Cluster 2 groups the factors that influence the decision of doing business in a sustainable way into three categories: micro-level drivers (i.e., the entrepreneur's personal values and ideals) (Gagnon, 2012), meso-level drivers (i.e., those related to markets and industries) (e.g., Hockerts & Wüstenhagen, 2010), and macro-level drivers (i.e., factors resulting from politics, legislation, and other institutions) (e.g., Schaltegger & Wagner, 2011). The third cluster comprises articles that address the strategic actions of ecologically sustainable firms, both focusing on the critical importance of the firm's business practices (i.e., ways in which a firm integrates environmental concerns into supply chain activities and operations, among others) (e.g., Marshall, McCarthy, McGrath, & Claudy, 2015) and their networking strategies with external stakeholders (i.e., the ability to build stable relationships with the external environment) (e.g., Kibler, Fink, Lang, & Muñoz, 2015). The fourth cluster reports the outcomes of ecologically sustainable entrepreneurship at macro-, meso-, and micro-levels. At the micro-level, articles deal with the primary goals that individuals aim at when creating and managing their sustainable enterprise (e.g., creating social and environmental value, instead of economic objectives solely) (e.g., Jolink & Niesten, 2015). At the meso-level, papers describe how sustainable firms drive the change towards sustainability in markets (e.g., York & Venkataraman, 2010); whereas, the way that sustainable firms, as role models, strive to improve the sustainability of the society as a whole is the core topic of studies at the macro-level (Parrish & Foxon, 2006). The articles in cluster 5 delve into the factors that enable ecologically sustainable entrepreneurship, shedding light on the role of business schools in shaping their academic offerings (e.g., curricula and courses) to promote the identification of sustainable business opportunities (e.g., Lourenço, Jones, & Jayawarna, 2013). Finally, cluster 6 highlights the financial challenges (i.e., raising financial resources from public and private investors) (e.g., Choi & Gray, 2008) and market barriers (e.g., the ethical reassignment of the entrepreneur might impede the correct development of the firm; consumer skepticism towards green and social ventures; among others) (e.g., Linnanen, 2002) for sustainable entrepreneurship. According to the authors, "the six clusters identified in the literature review indicate that research in ecological sustainable entrepreneurship mirrors the well-established process of entrepreneurship: opportunity discovery, creation and exploitation" (Gast et al., 2017, p. 52).

More recently, Muñoz and Cohen (2018) systematically reviewed 81 research articles published between 1995 and 2016. The pool of papers was retrieved from the WoS Database. After being screened via an iterative process, the sample was grouped and categorized by source and methodological approach. The authors reported two main streams of literature: the first brings sustainability into entrepreneurship, while the second one acts in the opposite manner. On one hand, the papers in the first group focused on the socio-political and ecological aspects that lead to a sustainable world. On the other hand, articles in the second group address "strategic, organizational, and market factors" (p. 303) which foster the rise of "competitive green companies and industries" (p. 303). Muñoz and Cohen (2018) built on Sahlman's (1996) work to provide a framework of four interrelated factors, namely "the sustainable entrepreneur", "the context for sustainable entrepreneurship", "the outcome of sustainable entrepreneurship (i.e., value creation), and "the sustainability opportunity". Articles pertaining to the first category—*the sustainable entrepreneur*—focus on the individual that leads the sustainable venture. Furthermore, six sub-themes are included in this category, which have been used by scholars as explanatory variables for the ability of entrepreneurs to recognize business opportunities connected to sustainable development. Among these, for example, scholars have acknowledged the entrepreneur's willingness to find an equilibrium between the two apparently opposed desires of making money and playing the sustainable entrepreneurship game (Schlange, 2006). The second category—*the context for sustainable entrepreneurship*—includes articles that deal with contextual factors (i.e., formal and informal elements that the entrepreneur cannot control but which affect the growth of the enterprise); for instance, support from formal institutions, especially in emerging sustainable markets (Dhanda & Murphy, 2011), and a supporting social context can foster or hinder the development of sustainable ventures (Muñoz & Dimov, 2015). The extant literature related to the *sustainable entrepreneurship outcome* is articulated in two sub-streams; namely, value creation and strategic returns. According to Muñoz and Cohen (2018), the leitmotif of this category deals with the "pays to be green hypothesis". More simply, sustainable ventures, thanks to their hybrid purpose (e.g., Doherty, Haugh, & Lyon, 2014)—that is, to reconcile wealth accumulation and sustainable development—are capable of simultaneously achieving financial outcomes while pursuing social and environmental goals. Finally, the *sustainability opportunities* category is comprised of the articles that focus on the ability of entrepreneurship to identify business opportunities under market imperfections (Cohen & Winn, 2007) or market failures (Dean & McMullen, 2007).

Each of the previous review studies has provided interesting insights into the field, but additional analysis of the literature using rigorous bibliometric tools can provide further understanding not previously fully grasped or evaluated. Only two reviews have contributed to the expansion of the knowledge with an objective approach (i.e., bibliometric analysis) (Sarango-Lalangui, Santos, & Hormiga, 2018; Terán-Yépez et al., 2020).

On one hand, Sarango-Lalangui et al. (2018) conducted a review shedding light on the most commonly used bibliometric performance indicators (i.e., the chronological trend of publications, the most prolific and cited authors, the top ten journals, and the most relevant articles), except from most prolific countries and institutions. However, the authors neglected to provide scientific maps of the linkages between the analyzed bibliometric indicators.

On the other hand, the most recent review on sustainable entrepreneurship addresses and fills this gap by graphically identifying (1) the main collaboration networks between countries and authors (co-citation analysis has been performed) and (2) the central research topics in the field, based on co-word analysis (Terán-Yépez et al., 2020). More specifically, the authors scrutinized the Scopus database from 2002 to 2018 and assessed the status of the literature on sustainable entrepreneurship by both looking at bibliometric performance indicators and scientific mapping over a sample of 216 articles. Most interestingly, the authors claimed that the literature can be divided into two sub-periods, each characterized by motor (i.e. well-developed and central in the literature), basic (i.e., transversal themes that are important for the research field but are internally undeveloped), emergent or decadent (i.e., weakly developed and marginal for the literature; these themes should be monitored to inspect future development or decline), and peripheral (i.e., marginal for the literature) themes. In particular, motor themes in the first sub-period (2002–2014) are *Sustainability* (pioneer papers in the field appear as an effort to mix sustainability and entrepreneurship theory) (e.g., Urbaniec, 2018), *Environmental Impact* (the focus of early documents was on strategies and practices to reduce the environmental impact of the activities of firms) (e.g., Keijzers, 2002), and *Development Strategy* (older articles often focused on the importance of promoting local development aimed at social and economic goals, in contrast to traditional economic development) (e.g., Rodríguez-Pose & Palavicini-Corona, 2013). Further, motor themes in the second sub-period (2015–2018) include the *Entrepreneur* (research is focused on the actors of sustainable development) (e.g., Munoz & Dimov, 2015), *Economic and Social Effects* (articles are focused on the importance of CSR as a precursor of sustainable entrepreneurship) (e.g., Sarango-Lalangui et al., 2018), *Environmental Entrepreneurship* (e.g., Thompson, Kiefer, & York, 2011), and *Developing Countries* (papers looking at sustainable performance of SMEs in developing economies) (e.g., Maas, Bunders, & Zweekhorst, 2015). As a final step of the review process, Terán-Yépez et al. (2020) provided a graphic map based on the co-occurrence of the most-used keywords in the papers. For instance, *sustainable entrepreneurship* was strongly linked to *sustainable development* which, together with other keywords (e.g., social entrepreneurship, environmental entrepreneurship, sustainable business, and entrepreneurial orientation), formed a standalone cluster that encompassed papers related to the principal theories on sustainable entrepreneurship. Further, the keyword *entrepreneur* was bound to *sustainability*, *SMEs*, and

Table 2.1 Review Studies on Sustainable Entrepreneurship in chronological order

	Source	Years Covered	Methodology	Papers	Results
1. Levinsohn (2013)	WoS	1999–2010	Critical	42	(a) The Green Emphasis; (b) The Individual; (c) Sustainable entrepreneurship as an expansion of entrepreneurship; (d) Sustainable entrepreneurship as a business opportunity; (e) Sustainable entrepreneurship as embedded; (f) Sustainable entrepreneurship as innovation; (g) Sustainable entrepreneurship in SMEs; (h) Extended discussion of Sustainable entrepreneurship concept; (i) Sustainable entrepreneurship as double bottom line; (j) Sustainable entrepreneurship as triple bottom line
2. Fellnhofer et al. (2014)	Scopus, EBSCO, EconLit, ingentaconnect, ScienceDirect, ABI/Inform Global/T&I ProQuest, Wiley Online Library, WoS, Google Scholar, SpringerLink, SSRN	Entire time span (up to 2013)	Systematic	218	(a) From social and environmental entrepreneurship to sustainable entrepreneurial innovation; (b) From an economic point of view to corporate sustainability; (c) Sustainability as an integral part of entrepreneurship
3. Aghelie et al. (2016)	–	1998–2012	Systematic	43	Describes and defines the concept of sustainable entrepreneurship

4. Greco and de Jong (2017)	WorldCat Discovery Service + Specific Journals	2011–2016 + older highly cited contributions	Narrative	132 (articles, books and theses)	Uncovers the definitions, main themes and methods that constitute the field of sustainable entrepreneurship
5. Gast et al. (2017)	ABI Informs/Pro Quest, EBSCOhost/ Business Source Premier, JSTOR, Science Direct, Springer Link, Wiley, Google Scholar	1996–2015	Systematic	114	(a) Drivers of engaging in sustainable entrepreneurship; (b) Drivers of conducting business in an ecologically sustainable way; (c) Strategic actions; (d) Outcomes of ecologically sustainable entrepreneurship; (e) Factors that enable ecologically sustainable entrepreneurship; (f) Challenges for ecologically sustainable entrepreneurship
6. Muñoz and Cohen (2018)	WoS	1995–2016	Systematic	81	(a) The entrepreneur; (b) The Context; (c) The Outcome; (d) The Opportunity
7. Sarango-Lalangui et al. (2018)	WoS	1956–2018	Bibliometric	282	(a) Chronological trend; (b) Most prolific and cited authors; (c) Top 10 journals; (d) Most relevant articles
8. Terán-Yépez et al. (2020)	Scopus	2002–2018	Bibliometric (co-citation analysis)	216	(a) Most common bibliometric performance indicators; (b) Scientific map of collaboration network between countries and authors; (c) Diagram of main researched themes

Source: author's elaboration

business development, presumably because the individual (i.e., the sustainable entrepreneur) is the principal actor that can promote the change towards sustainability, thanks to his/her ability to recognize sustainable business opportunities in the market. Finally, *innovation* leads a cluster that ties together articles that use *business model*, *start-ups*, and *corporate sustainability* as preferred keywords. Unsurprisingly, innovation is a key driver for sustainable entrepreneurship, as it enables the identification of new business opportunities inspired by the need to pursue social, environmental, and economic goals.

To conclude, the abovementioned reviews have acknowledged several themes and issues covered within the research literature (Table 2.1). However, as many scholars, practitioners, and institutions have shown increasing interest in sustainable entrepreneurship, this field has been experiencing a continuous flourishing growth. As a consequence, there is a need to regularly conduct new review studies to assess the evolution of the field; that is, by highlighting past achievements, capturing current gaps, and delineating promising future research directions (e.g., Terán-Yépez et al., 2020)

References

Abrahamsson, A. (2003). *Researching Sustainopreneurship–Conditions, Concepts, Approaches, Arenas and Questions*. 13th International Sustainable Development Research Conference.

Aghelie, A., Sorooshian, S., & Azizan, N. A. (2016). Research Gap in Sustainopreneurship. *Indian Journal of Science and Technology, 9*(12), 1–6. https://doi.org/10.17485/ijst/2016/v9i12/77648

Atiq, M., & Karatas-Ozkan, M. (2013). Sustainable Corporate Entrepreneurship from a Strategic Corporate Social Responsibility Perspective. *International Journal of Entrepreneurship and Innovation, 14*(1), 5–14. Scopus. https://doi.org/10.5367/ijei.2013.0102

Bocken, N. M. P. (2015). Sustainable Venture Capital—Catalyst for Sustainable Start-Up Success? *Journal of Cleaner Production, 108*, 647–658. Scopus. https://doi.org/10.1016/j.jclepro.2015.05.079

Choi, D. Y., & Gray, E. R. (2008). The Venture Development Processes of "Sustainable" Entrepreneurs. *Management Research News, 31*(8), 558–569. Scopus. https://doi.org/10.1108/01409170810892127

Cohen, B., & Winn, M. I. (2007). Market Imperfections, Opportunity and Sustainable Entrepreneurship. *Journal of Business Venturing, 22*(1), 29–49. Scopus. https://doi.org/10.1016/j.jbusvent.2004.12.001

Dean, T. J., & McMullen, J. S. (2007). Toward a Theory of Sustainable Entrepreneurship: Reducing Environmental Degradation Through Entrepreneurial Action. *Journal of Business Venturing, 22*(1), 50–76. Scopus. https://doi.org/10.1016/j.jbusvent.2005.09.003

Dhanda, K. K., & Murphy, P. J. (2011). The New Wild West Is Green: Carbon Offset Markets, Transactions, and Providers. *Academy of Management Perspectives, 25*(4), 37–49. https://doi.org/10.5465/amp.2009.0110

Doherty, B., Haugh, H., & Lyon, F. (2014). Social Enterprises as Hybrid Organizations: A Review and Research Agenda. *International Journal of Management Reviews, 16*(4), 417–436. https://doi.org/10.1111/ijmr.12028

Fellnhofer, K., Kraus, S., & Bouncken, R. B. (2014). The Current State of Research on Sustainable Entrepreneurship. *International Journal of Business Research, 14*(3), 163–172. Scopus. https://doi.org/10.18374/IJBR-14-3.11

Gagnon, M. A. (2012). Sustainable Minded Entrepreneurs: Developing and Testing a Values-Based Framework. *Journal of Strategic Innovation and Sustainability, 8*(1), 17.

Gast, J., Gundolf, K., & Cesinger, B. (2017). Doing Business in a Green Way: A Systematic Review of the Ecological Sustainability Entrepreneurship Literature and Future Research Directions. *Journal of Cleaner Production, 147*, 44–56. https://doi.org/10.1016/j.jclepro.2017.01.065

Gibbs, D. (2006). Sustainability Entrepreneurs, Ecopreneurs and the Development of a Sustainable Economy. *Greener Management International, 2006*(55), 63–78. https://doi.org/10.9774/GLEAF.3062.2006.au.00007

Greco, A., & de Jong, G. (2017). *Sustainable Entrepreneurship: Definitions, Themes and Research Gaps*. Working Paper Series 1706-CSE, University of Groningen. Retrieved from https://www.rug.nl/cf/pdfs/cse/wps6_angela.pdf

Hall, J. K., Daneke, G. A., & Lenox, M. J. (2010). Sustainable Development and Entrepreneurship: Past Contributions and Future Directions. *Journal of Business Venturing, 25*(5), 439–448. https://doi.org/10.1016/j.jbusvent.2010.01.002

Hart, S., & Christensen, C. M. (2002). The great leap: Driving innovation from the base of the pyramid. *MIT Sloan Management Review, 44*(1), 51–56.

Hockerts, K., & Wüstenhagen, R. (2010). Greening Goliaths Versus Emerging Davids—Theorizing About the Role of Incumbents and New Entrants in Sustainable Entrepreneurship. *Journal of Business Venturing, 25*(5), 481–492. https://doi.org/10.1016/j.jbusvent.2009.07.005

Jolink, A., & Niesten, E. (2015). Sustainable Development and Business Models of Entrepreneurs in the Organic Food Industry. *Business Strategy and the Environment, 24*(6), 386–401. https://doi.org/10.1002/bse.1826

Keijzers, G. (2002). The Transition to the Sustainable Enterprise. *Journal of Cleaner Production, 10*(4), 349–359. Scopus. https://doi.org/10.1016/S0959-6526(01)00051-8

Kibler, E., Fink, M., Lang, R., & Muñoz, P. (2015). Place Attachment and Social Legitimacy: Revisiting the Sustainable Entrepreneurship Journey. *Journal of Business Venturing Insights, 3*, 24–29. Scopus. https://doi.org/10.1016/j.jbvi.2015.04.001

Kirkwood, J., & Walton, S. (2010). What Motivates Ecopreneurs to Start Businesses? *International Journal of Entrepreneurial Behavior & Research, 16*(3), 204–228. https://doi.org/10.1108/13552551011042799.

Lans, T., Blok, V., & Wesselink, R. (2014). Learning Apart and Together: Towards an Integrated Competence Framework for Sustainable Entrepreneurship in Higher Education. *Journal of Cleaner Production, 62*, 37–47. Scopus. https://doi.org/10.1016/j.jclepro.2013.03.036

Levinsohn, D. (2013). Disembedded and Beheaded?—A Critical Review of the Emerging Field of Sustainability Entrepreneurship. *International Journal of Entrepreneurship and Small Business, 19*(2), 190. https://doi.org/10.1504/IJESB.2013.054963

Linnanen, L. (2002). An Insider's Experiences with Environmental Entrepreneurship. *Greener Management International, 2002*(38), 71–80. https://doi.org/10.9774/GLEAF.3062.2002.su.00008

Lourenço, F., Jones, O., & Jayawarna, D. (2013). Promoting Sustainable Development: The Role of Entrepreneurship Education. *International Small Business Journal, 31*(8), 841–865. https://doi.org/10.1177/0266242611435825

Maas, J., Bunders, J. F. G., & Zweekhorst, M. B. M. (2015). Trust building and entrepreneurial behaviour in a distrusting environment: A longitudinal study from Bangladesh. *International Journal of Business and Globalisation, 14*(1), 75–96. Scopus. https://doi.org/10.1504/IJBG.2015.066100

Marshall, D., McCarthy, L., McGrath, P., & Claudy, M. C. (2015). Going Above and Beyond: How Sustainability Culture and Entrepreneurial Orientation Drive Social Sustainability Supply Chain Practice Adoption. *Supply Chain Management: An International Journal, 20*(4), 434–454. https://doi.org/10.1108/SCM-08-2014-0267

Miller, T. L., & Wesley, Curtis I. (2010). Assessing Mission and Resources for Social Change: An Organizational Identity Perspective on Social Venture Capitalists' Decision Criteria: *Entrepreneurship Theory and Practice*. Retrieved from https://journals.sagepub.com/doi/10.1111/j.1540-6520.2010.00388.x

Moore, S. B., & Manring, S. L. (2009). Strategy Development in Small and Medium Sized Enterprises for Sustainability and Increased Value Creation. *Journal of Cleaner Production, 17*(2), 276–282. https://doi.org/10.1016/j.jclepro.2008.06.004

Muñoz, P., & Cohen, B. (2018). Sustainable Entrepreneurship Research: Taking Stock and Looking Ahead. *Business Strategy and the Environment, 27*(3), 300–322. Scopus. https://doi.org/10.1002/bse.2000

Muñoz, P., & Dimov, D. (2015). The Call of the Whole in Understanding the Development of Sustainable Ventures. *Journal of Business Venturing, 30*(4), 632–654. Scopus. https://doi.org/10.1016/j.jbusvent.2014.07.012

Munoz, P., & Dimov, D. (2015). The Call of the Whole in Understanding the Development of Sustainable Ventures. *Journal of Business Venturing, 30*(4), 632–654. https://doi.org/10.1016/j.jbusvent.2014.07.012

Parrish, B. D. (2010). Sustainability-driven entrepreneurship: Principles of organization design. *Journal of Business Venturing, 25*, 510–523.

Parrish, B. D., & Foxon, T. J. (2006). Sustainability Entrepreneurship and Equitable Transitions to a Low-Carbon Economy. *Greener Management International, 55*, 47–62. JSTOR.

Pinkse, J., & Groot, K. (2015). Sustainable Entrepreneurship and Corporate Political Activity: Overcoming Market Barriers in the Clean Energy Sector. *Entrepreneurship: Theory and Practice, 39*(3), 633–654. Scopus. https://doi.org/10.1111/etap.12055

Rodríguez-Pose, A., & Palavicini-Corona, E. I. (2013). Does Local Economic Development Really Work? Assessing LED Across Mexican Municipalities. *Geoforum, 44*, 303–315. https://doi.org/10.1016/j.geoforum.2012.07.010

Sahlman, W. A. (1996). Some Thoughts on Business Plans. In W. A. Sahlman, H. Stevenson, M. J. Roberts, & A. V. Bhide (Eds.), *The Entrepreneurial Venture* (pp. 138–176). Cambridge, MA: Harvard Business School Press.

Sarango-Lalangui, P., Santos, J., & Hormiga, E. (2018). The Development of Sustainable Entrepreneurship Research Field. *Sustainability, 10*(6), 2005. https://doi.org/10.3390/su10062005

Schaltegger, S., & Wagner, M. (2011). Sustainable Entrepreneurship and Sustainability Innovation: Categories and Interactions. *Business Strategy and the Environment, 20*(4), 222–237. Scopus. https://doi.org/10.1002/bse.682

Schlange, L. (2006). *What Drives Sustainable Entrepreneurs?* Applied Business and Entrepreneurship Association International Conference, Kona, Hawaii.

Spence, M., Ben Boubaker Gherib, J., & Biwolé, V. O. (2011). Sustainable Entrepreneurship: Is Entrepreneurial Will Enough? A North-South Comparison. *Journal of Business Ethics, 99*(3), 335–367. Scopus. https://doi.org/10.1007/s10551-010-0656-1

Terán-Yépez, E., Marín-Carrillo, G. M., del Pilar Casado-Belmonte, M., & de las Mercedes Capobianco-Uriarte, M. (2020). Sustainable Entrepreneurship: Review of Its Evolution and New Trends. *Journal of Cleaner Production, 252*, 119742. https://doi.org/10.1016/j.jclepro.2019.119742

Thompson, N., Kiefer, K., & York, J. G. (2011). Distinctions Not Dichotomies: Exploring Social, Sustainable, and Environmental Entrepreneurship. In G. T. Lumpkin & J. A. Katz (A c. Di) (Eds.), *Advances in Entrepreneurship, Firm Emergence and Growth* (Vol. 13, pp. 201–229). Bingley: Emerald Group Publishing Limited. https://doi.org/10.1108/S1074-7540(2011)0000013012

Tilley, F., & Parrish, B. D. (2006). From Poles to Wholes: Facilitating an Integrated Approach to Sustainable Entrepreneurship. *World Review of Entrepreneurship, Management and Sustainable Development, 2*(4), 281–294. Scopus. https://doi.org/10.1504/WREMSD.2006.010214

Urbaniec, M. (2018). Sustainable Entrepreneurship: Innovation-Related Activities in European Enterprises. *Polish Journal of Environmental Studies, 27*(4), 1773–1779. https://doi.org/10.15244/pjoes/78155

York, J. G., & Venkataraman, S. (2010). The Entrepreneur–Environment Nexus: Uncertainty, Innovation, and Allocation. *Journal of Business Venturing, 25*(5), 449–463. https://doi.org/10.1016/j.jbusvent.2009.07.007

Chapter 3
The Review Approach

A literature review typically maps the theoretical boundaries of a research field with the triple aim of taking stock of a research domain, identifying its gaps, and delineating the most promising future lines of research.

To track a field's intellectual realm, objective and subjective approaches can be alternatively or jointly applied. Objective approaches to literature reviews apply bibliographic quantitative methodologies (e.g., citation analysis) and are often software-based (Di Stefano, Peteraf, & Verona, 2010; Galvagno, 2011); whereas subjective ones utilize qualitative methodologies, such as systematic literature reviews (Tranfield, Denyer, & Smart, 2003). On one hand, objective approaches have been increasingly adopted in review studies, including sustainability issues (Zhang et al., 2017, 2019). To this extent, objective approaches enhance the probability to observe latent and unexpected connections between diverse literature streams. This approach is especially valued by researchers, as it allows them to overcome the cognitive biases ingrained in subjective methodologies (e.g., a researcher pointing out the features of a research field in which they are more familiar with or an expert in). On the other hand, subjective approaches still successfully meet the needs of researchers to produce systematical critiques of a research field. Therefore, unsurprisingly, researchers now acknowledge the complementary capacity of objective and subjective methodologies to enable a more comprehensive understanding of the structure and specific characteristics of any research field (e.g., Ardito, Scuotto, Del Giudice, & Petruzzelli, 2019).

Accordingly, this study uses a mixed approach (i.e., objective and subjective) to take stock of the current knowledge, to detect the research gaps, and to delineate the research agenda in the research domain of sustainable entrepreneurship. In particular, to inspect and classify the literature on sustainable entrepreneurship, we conducted a structured literature review which relied on bibliometric analysis as the objective approach (i.e., bibliometric performance indicators analysis and network analysis by means of bibliographic coupling maps) and performed content analysis as the subjective approach, in order to qualitatively assess the articles

M. Pinna, *Sustainable Entrepreneurship*, SpringerBriefs in Business,
https://doi.org/10.1007/978-3-030-57818-3_3

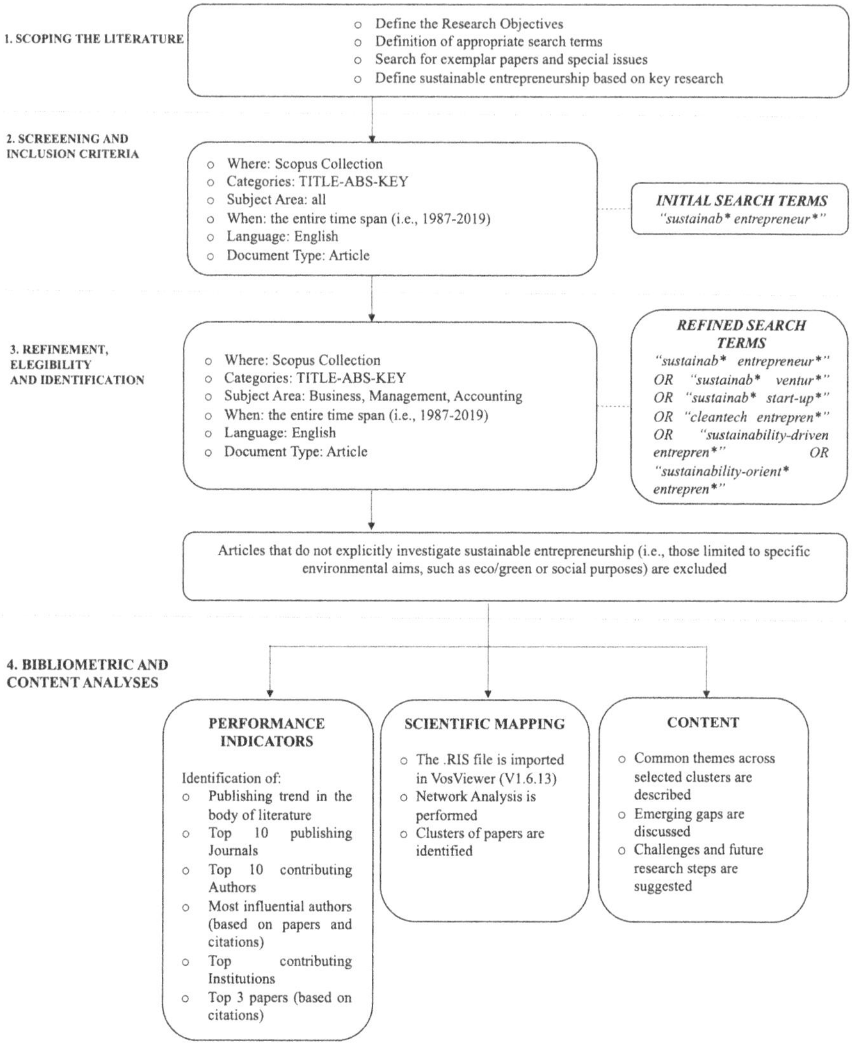

Fig. 3.1 The review process. (Source: Author's elaboration)

displayed in the map. Specifically, a four-step procedure was adopted (Fahimnia, Sarkis, & Davarzani, 2015) and adapted for the purposes of this study.[1] The four aforementioned steps entailed (see Fig. 3.1):

1. The definition of the appropriate search terms;

[1]Fahimnia's et al. (2015) routine slightly differed, in the way that the initial bibliometric statistics stood alone in Step 4, while more sophisticated bibliometric analyses and the scientific mapping were addressed in Step 5.

2. The screening of initial search results;
3. The refinement of search results;
4. The conduction of Bibliometric (Bibliometric Performance Indicators and Scientific Mapping) and Content analyses.

Section 3.1 details steps 1 to 3, while Sect. 3.2 comprises step 4.

3.1 The Search, Screening, and Refinement Procedure

This study relies on the Scopus Database. This database is the broadest abstract and citation collection of peer-reviewed scientific documents across all research fields. The Scopus database has been widely used in numerous literature reviews for business and management review studies, as it includes far more titles than the Web of Science database), thus allowing a complete overview of a research domain.

To identify the best search strategy, the screening routine of David and Han (2004) was followed. To begin, a preliminary search of the terms "*sustainab* entrepreneur*[2]*" within the categories "Title, Abstract and Keywords" identified 476 peer-reviewed academic documents (of which, 315 were in the area of Business, Management, and Accounting and 106 were available in Open Access). Afterward, the query string was adjusted to ensure that all relevant topics in the sustainable entrepreneurship literature were fully covered by the selected keywords. In particular, the search term *"sustainab* entrepreneur*"* was complemented with several additional keywords related to the field of sustainable entrepreneurship and venturing; for example, *"sustainab* ventur*"*. As sustainability pursues both environmental and social goals, but is limited to neither specific environmental aims (eco or green) or social purposes, the search strategy deliberately omitted the following terms: *"Green"*, *"Ecolog*"*, *"Environment*"*, and *"Social"*.

The search procedure yielded a sample of 195 peer-reviewed articles in the English language, within all the thematic categories (e.g., Business and Management, Social Sciences, Computer Sciences, etc.). Eventually, the articles within the "Business, Management and Accounting" category were searched over the entire time span available (1987–2019).[3] The final search string adopted was the following: TITLE-ABS-KEY ("sustainab* entrepreneur*" OR "sustainab* ventur*" OR "sustainab* start-up*" OR "cleantech entrepren*" OR "sustainability-driven entrepren*" OR "sustainability-orient* entrepren*") AND (LIMIT-TO (DOCTYPE,

[2]The symbol "*" indicates that variations on the ending of the word are allowed; for instance, by selecting "entrepren*", the search engine returns words like entrepreneurship, entrepreneur, entrepreneurial, etc.

[3]Articles published in 2020 were deliberately excluded, in order to compare complete years. However, in light of the use of citations in this study, it is worth underlining that citations received up until April 20, 2020 are included.

"ar")) AND (LIMIT-TO (SUBJAREA, "BUSI")) AND (LIMIT-TO (LANGUAGE, "English")).

By screening the Scopus Database, after reading all the abstracts, a set of 166 articles was obtained. The search results were saved in .RIS format to include all the essential paper information, such as paper title, author names and affiliations, abstract, keywords, and references. As a further check, to make sure no double entries or accidental search results were included in the final sample, a refinement procedure (e.g., removal of duplicates, papers with unknown author names or missing bibliometric information) was performed in Zotero. The final sample was made up of 166 peer-reviewed articles. To create the corresponding refinements in the .RIS file, the data in Zotero was reconverted to .RIS. The resulting .RIS file was then imported in Publish or Perish[4] Version 6, in order to obtain the citations of the sample, which were used to select the papers to be included in subsequent analyses.

3.2 The Research Methodology

3.2.1 Bibliometrics

The area of research that uses the information comprised in scientific publications has been defined as 'bibliometrics'. Bibliometrics "indicate the collection, the handling and the analysis of quantitative bibliographic data, derived from scientific publications" (Verbeek, Debackere, Luwel, & Zimmermann, 2002, p. 181). The aim of bibliometrics is to detect tendencies within a discipline (De Bakker, Groenewegen, & Den Hond, 2005) by looking at an author's scientific output, in terms of both documents and citations (Verbeek et al., 2002).

Broadly speaking, bibliometric analysis consists of two techniques: *bibliometric performance indicators* and *scientific mapping* (Terán-Yépez, Marín-Carrillo, del Pilar Casado-Belmonte, & de las Mercedes Capobianco-Uriarte, 2020). On one hand, bibliometric performance indicators favor the identification of the performance of authors, journals, institutions, and countries (e.g., the number of articles, citations, average citations per article, h-index, and so on). Indeed, this technique has been recognized as "a guide to the status of research", as it provides useful information for experts seeking to evaluate the scientific activities within a research field (e.g., Rey-Martí, Ribeiro-Soriano, & Palacios-Marqués, 2016).

On the other hand, scientific mapping relies on network theory to explore the structure of a field (Liu, Yin, Liu, & Dunford, 2015). To help researchers to visualize patterns and trends in the scientific literature, a wide range of science mapping

[4]Publish or Perish is a software program that retrieves and analyzes academic citations and returns several useful metrics, such as (1) the total number of papers and total number of citations; (2) average citations per paper, citations per author, papers per author, and citations per year; and (3) Hirsch's h-index and related parameters; among others.

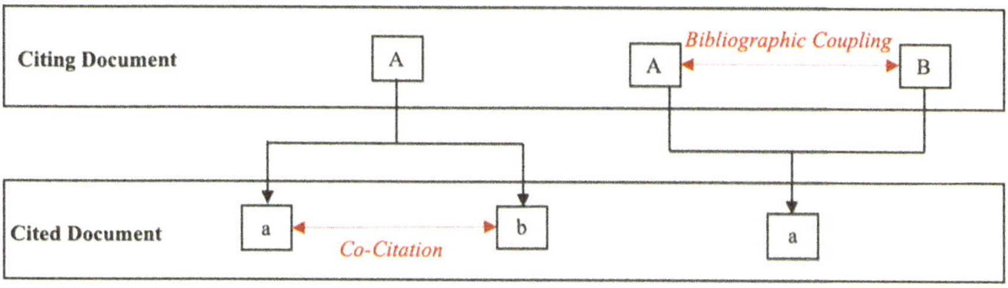

Fig. 3.2 Differences between co-citation and bibliographic coupling methods. (Source: Vogel & Güttel, 2013)

software tools (e.g., CiteSpace, VosViewer, and others) have been developed. In particular, these graphic maps are composed of clusters of articles which group together common facets of the literature (i.e., research topics, countries, institutions, journals, authors, and keywords). More simply, if two or more papers are in the same cluster, each article is linked to the other articles within the cluster. To this extent, scientific mapping is a useful tool for scholars to identify relevant clusters, visualize the linking networks, and assess the extent to which they are connected (Liu et al., 2015). Scientific mapping can be also performed by relying on more sophisticated methods, such as co-citation analysis and bibliographic coupling (e.g., Vogel & Güttel, 2013), which have been proven as powerful tools for detecting both old and new topical areas (e.g., Fahimnia et al., 2015). Over the past five decades, *co-citation analysis* and *bibliographic coupling* have ruled bibliometrics as the most reliable tools to perform scientific literature reviews (Vogel & Güttel, 2013). At a glance, these two citation-based methods might look alike; however, there are considerable differences between them. Co-citation is defined as "the frequency with which two documents are cited together in the same reference list", whereas bibliographic coupling happens when "two documents have at least one reference in common" (Vogel & Güttel, 2013, p. 428). Figure 3.2 shows that documents are co-cited if they appear together in the reference list of a publication, whereas two citing documents are coupled if they share at least one reference. Hence, the preference between these two methodologies refers to the "analytical scope" (Vogel & Güttel, 2013, p. 428) of the researcher: co-citation captures the "classics" of a research field (i.e., the older the document, the wider the amount of time the publication has to obtain citations); while bibliographic coupling detects the current trends in the literature (i.e., documents are considered independently from the number of citations). More simply, co-citation focuses on the consumption process of older *cited* documents, while bibliographic coupling concentrates the production of younger *citing* ones. In light of this, these two methodologies complement, rather than substitute, each other.

3.2.2 *Qualitative Content Analysis*

As a first step, after reading the paper abstract, the author assigned a category label to each cluster. Then, the author asked one senior researcher—an expert in the field of social and sustainable entrepreneurship—to discuss the category labels she previously assigned and to identify a shared solution to name each cluster. Further, to qualitatively assess the content of the papers in each cluster, the articles were entirely read and manually catalogued by the author. To fulfil this aim, a bibliographic note card was created to summarize the *purpose*, the *typology* (whether the paper was theoretical, empirical, or a literature review), the *methodology* (whether empirical papers relied on quantitative, qualitative, or mixed methodologies), the type of *analyses* performed (e.g., OLS regression, SEM), and the *findings* of each paper.

Considering the benefits of performing both bibliometric techniques (Small, 1999), this volume relies on bibliometric performance indicators and scientific mapping to scrutinize the intellectual field of sustainable entrepreneurship. From a methodological standpoint, bibliographic coupling was applied to perform scientific mapping. In fact, to the extent that sustainable entrepreneurship is a recent and rapidly growing research field, bibliographic coupling is the ideal methodology, as it provides interesting insights by looking not only at the core of the field (i.e., citations and co-citations), but also at the frontiers of knowledge (i.e., bibliographic coupling), especially "in subject areas characterized by vibrant publication activity" (Vogel & Güttel, 2013, p. 429). In this sense, this study complements the previous literature reviews of sustainable entrepreneurship, especially the co-citation analysis recently conducted by Terán-Yépez et al. (2020) and the systematic review published by Muñoz and Cohen (2018). Practically, the scientific mapping was carried out using VosViewer, a scientifically accepted tool for the visualization of scientific maps. This software allows the user to graphically identify and understand the linkages between documents, citations, countries, institutions, journals, authors, and keywords (Castillo-Vergara, Alvarez-Marin, & Placencio-Hidalgo, 2018). As a third step, a qualitative assessment of the research production of sustainable entrepreneurship is conducted through content analysis. Finally, the conjoint adoption of bibliometrics and content analysis enabled a systematic and comprehensive understanding of the status of sustainable entrepreneurship research.

References

Ardito, L., Scuotto, V., Del Giudice, M., & Petruzzelli, A. M. (2019). A Bibliometric Analysis of Research on Big Data Analytics for Business and Management. *Management Decision, 57*(8), 1993–2009. https://doi.org/10.1108/MD-07-2018-0754

Castillo-Vergara, M., Alvarez-Marin, A., & Placencio-Hidalgo, D. (2018). A Bibliometric Analysis of Creativity in the Field of Business Economics. *Journal of Business Research, 85*, 1–9. https://doi.org/10.1016/j.jbusres.2017.12.011

David, R. J., & Han, S.-K. (2004). A Systematic Assessment of the Empirical Support for Transaction Cost Economics. *Strategic Management Journal, 25*(1), 39–58. https://doi.org/10.1002/smj.359

De Bakker, F. G. A., Groenewegen, P., & Den Hond, F. (2005). A bibliometric analysis of 30 years of research and theory on corporate social responsibility and corporate social performance. *Business & Society, 44*(3), 283–317. https://doi.org/10.1177/0007650305278086

Di Stefano, G., Peteraf, M., & Verona, G. (2010). Dynamic Capabilities Deconstructed: A Bibliographic Investigation Into the Origins, Development, and Future Directions of the Research Domain. *Industrial and Corporate Change, 19*(4), 1187–1204. https://doi.org/10.1093/icc/dtq027

Fahimnia, B., Sarkis, J., & Davarzani, H. (2015). Green Supply Chain Management: A Review and Bibliometric Analysis. *International Journal of Production Economics, 162*, 101–114. https://doi.org/10.1016/j.ijpe.2015.01.003

Galvagno, M. (2011). The Intellectual Structure of the Anti-Consumption and Consumer Resistance Field: An Author Co-Citation Analysis. *European Journal of Marketing, 45*(11/12), 1688–1701. https://doi.org/10.1108/03090561111167441

Liu, Z., Yin, Y., Liu, W., & Dunford, M. (2015). Visualizing the Intellectual Structure and Evolution of Innovation Systems Research: A Bibliometric Analysis. *Scientometrics, 103*(1), 135–158. https://doi.org/10.1007/s11192-014-1517-y

Muñoz, P., & Cohen, B. (2018). Sustainable Entrepreneurship Research: Taking Stock and Looking Ahead. *Business Strategy and the Environment, 27*(3), 300–322. Scopus. https://doi.org/10.1002/bse.2000

Rey-Martí, A., Ribeiro-Soriano, D., & Palacios-Marqués, D. (2016). A Bibliometric Analysis of Social Entrepreneurship. *Journal of Business Research, 69*(5), 1651–1655. https://doi.org/10.1016/j.jbusres.2015.10.033

Small, H. (1999). Visualizing Science by Citation Mapping. *Journal of the American Society for Information Science, 50*(9), 799–813. https://doi.org/10.1002/(SICI)1097-4571

Terán-Yépez, E., Marín-Carrillo, G. M., del Pilar Casado-Belmonte, M., & de las Mercedes Capobianco-Uriarte, M. (2020). Sustainable Entrepreneurship: Review of Its Evolution and New Trends. *Journal of Cleaner Production, 252*, 119742. https://doi.org/10.1016/j.jclepro.2019.119742

Tranfield, D., Denyer, D., & Smart, P. (2003). Towards a Methodology for Developing Evidence-Informed Management Knowledge by Means of Systematic Review. *British Journal of Management, 14*(3), 207–222. https://doi.org/10.1111/1467-8551.00375

Verbeek, A., Debackere, K., Luwel, M., & Zimmermann, E. (2002). Measuring Progress and Evolution in Science and Technology—I: The Multiple Uses of Bibliometric Indicators. *International Journal of Management Reviews, 4*(2), 179–211. https://doi.org/10.1111/1468-2370.00083

Vogel, R., & Güttel, W. H. (2013). The Dynamic Capability View in Strategic Management: A Bibliometric Review: DCV in Strategic Management. *International Journal of Management Reviews, 15*, 426–446. https://doi.org/10.1111/ijmr.12000

Zhang, Y., Huang, K., Yu, Y., & Yang, B. (2017). Mapping of water footprint research: A bibliometric analysis during 2006–2015. *Journal of Cleaner Production, 149*, 70–79. https://doi.org/10.1016/j.jclepro.2017.02.067

Zhang, C., Fang, Y., Chen, X., & Congshan, T. (2019). Bibliometric analysis of trends in global sustainable livelihood research. *Sustainability, 11*(4), 1150. https://doi.org/10.3390/su11041150

Chapter 4
The Evolution and Distribution of the Scientific Knowledge

4.1 Bibliometric Performance Indicators

The analysis of the contributions published in a specific field of research allows us to frame the boundaries of the field itself, to identify any possible gaps in knowledge, and to inspect the most promising lines of future research. More simply, scientific production research orients researchers to quickly grasp what has been done, what is missing, and what needs to be further investigated in a research field.

This chapter provides an overview of the distribution of sustainable entrepreneurship research by looking at descriptive results. Specifically, this chapter shows the total amount of articles published, the most influential journals and papers, and the most prolific authors, institutions, and countries.

Table 4.1 illustrates the metrics of the sample over the last 17 years. Overall, the field of sustainable entrepreneurship accounts for 166 papers, generating a total amount of 5611 citations (311.72 per year) and developing a global H-Index of 30. Further, each paper received an average of 33.80 citations and each author was cited 2962.15 times.

4.1.1 The Evolution of the Scientific Production

Figure 4.1 shows the trend in the number of published articles. According to the data, the history of sustainable entrepreneurship dates back to 2002. From 2002 until 2014, the number of publications was fairly low (M = 3.15 papers published per year). From 2015 to 2019, the number of peer-reviewed articles skyrocketed (+75%), resulting in a geometric growth of the field. Looking at the data, a sharp increase was reported from 2017 to 2018, where the number of contributions doubled in size. Indeed, a few special issues on sustainable entrepreneurship

M. Pinna, *Sustainable Entrepreneurship*, SpringerBriefs in Business,
https://doi.org/10.1007/978-3-030-57818-3_4

Table 4.1 Overall citation counts

	Counts
Papers	166
Citations	5611
Cites_Year	311.72
Cites_Paper	33.80
Cites_Author	2962.15
Papers_Author	85.32
Authors_Paper	2.42
h_index	30

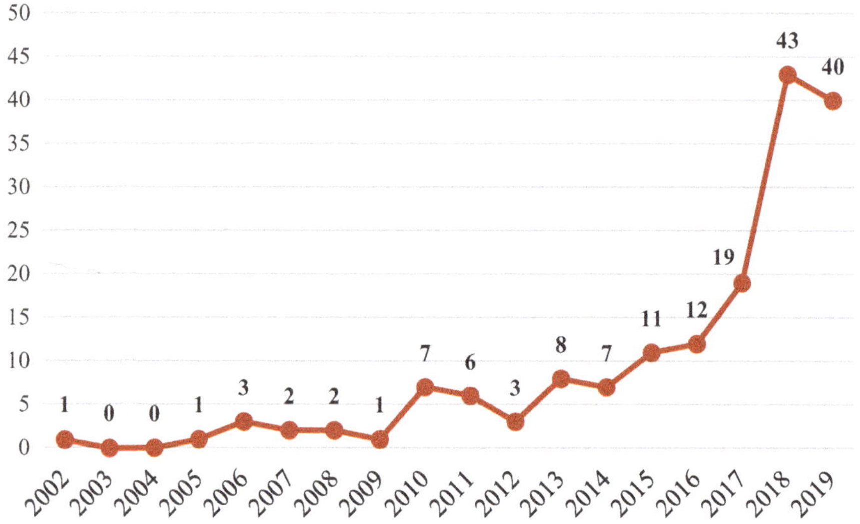

Fig. 4.1 Publishing trend in the field of sustainable entrepreneurship

appeared, in 2010, in the Journal of Business Venturing (Volume 25, Issue 5) and, in 2018, in the International Journal of Entrepreneurial Venturing (Volume 10, Issue 2). Another special issue from Small Business Economics (Volume 52, Issue 4) was promoted and published in 2019.

4.1.2 Journals, Authors, and Institutions

It should be noted that 67 journals contributed to the publication of the 166 identified papers. In particular, 10 journals hosted 92 of the total articles, representing 55% of the entire sample. Table 4.2 shows the list of journals in which these papers appeared, by year, in order of contributions. Furthermore, the Journal of Cleaner Production (29 published articles), Journal of Business Venturing (11 articles), and

Table 4.2 Journal list by year (contributions order)

N.	Source	Year																		Total	Special Issue
		2002	2003	2004	2005	2006	2007	2008	2009	2010	2011	2012	2013	2014	2015	2016	2017	2018	2019		
1	*J of Cleaner Production*	1								1			1	1	3	3	3	8	7	29	
2	*J of Business Venturing*						2			5					1		1	1	1	11	*
3	*Business Strategy and the Environment*					2		1			1					1	2	2		9	
4	*Int J of Entrepreneurial Behaviour and Research*																9		9		
5	*Small Business Economics*																	1	8	9	*
6	*Int J of Entrepreneurship and Small Business*										2	1			1	1	1			6	
7	*Organization and Environment*														1	1	1	1	2	6	
8	*Int J of Entrepreneurial Venturing*																	5		5	*
9	*Entrepreneurship and Sustainability Issues*																	2	2	4	
10	*Entrepreneurship: Theory and Practice*										1				1				2	4	
11	*J of Business Ethics*										1								2	3	
12	*Business Strategy and Development*																	2		2	
13	*Corporate Governance (Bingley)*												1				1			2	
14	*Entrepreneurial Business and Economics Review*														1			1	2		
15	*Industry and Higher Education*															2				2	

(continued)

Table 4.2 (continued)

N.	Source	Year																		Total	Special Issue
		2002	2003	2004	2005	2006	2007	2008	2009	2010	2011	2012	2013	2014	2015	2016	2017	2018	2019		
16	*Int Entrepreneurship and Management J*																	2		2	
17	*Int J of Business and Globalisation*														1				1	2	
18	*Int J of Business and Society*																	1	1	2	
19	*Int J of Entrepreneurship and Innovation*												1						1	2	
20	*Int J of Entrepreneurship and Innovation Management*																		2	2	
21	*J of Business Venturing Insights*														1		1			2	
22	*J of Small Business and Enterprise Development*							1									1		2		
23	*J of Small Business and Entrepreneurship*											1					1			2	
24	*J of Small Business Management*																	1	1	2	
25	*Strategic Change*																	1	1	2	
26	*World Review of Entrepreneurship, Management and Sustainable Development*					1								1						2	
27	*Academy of Management J*												1							1	
28	*Advances in Culture, Tourism and Hospitality Research*											1								1	
29	*Annals of Tourism Research*																1			1	

30	*Asia Pacific J of Tourism Research*											1							1	
31	*Asian J of Management Cases*											1							1	
32	*Australasian Marketing J*															1			1	
33	*British Food J*																	1	1	
34	*Business and Society*															1			1	
35	*Business Horizons*									1									1	
36	*Corporate Social Responsibility and Environmental Management*								1										1	
37	*DLSU Business and Economics Review*																	1	1	
38	*Emerald Emerging Markets Case Studies*																	1	1	
39	*Entrepreneurship and Regional Development*												1						1	
40	*EuroMed J of Business*												1						1	
41	*Gender in Management*															1			1	
42	*Global Business and Organizational Excellence*															1			1	
43	*Innovation*															1			1	
44	*Int J of Business Research*												1						1	
45	*Int J of E-Entrepreneurship and Innovation*																	1	1	
46	*Int J of Entrepreneurship*																	1	1	
47	*Int J of Information Systems in the Service Sector*											1						1		

(continued)

Table 4.2 (continued)

N.	Source	Year																		Total	Special Issue
		2002	2003	2004	2005	2006	2007	2008	2009	2010	2011	2012	2013	2014	2015	2016	2017	2018	2019		
48	*Int J of Management Education*															1				1	
49	*Int J of Trade and Global Markets*																1			1	
50	*Int Small Business J: Researching Entrepreneurship*														1					1	
51	*J for Int Business and Entrepreneurship Development*																	1		1	
52	*J of Business Strategy*																		1	1	
53	*J of Developmental Entrepreneurship*																	1		1	
54	*J of Enterprising Communities*																	1		1	
55	*J of Entrepreneurship*																	1		1	
56	*J of Entrepreneurship and Public Policy*																		1	1	
57	*J of Family Business Strategy*																1			1	
58	*J of Place Management and Development*													1						1	
59	*J of Technology Management and Innovation*												1							1	
60	*J on Chain and Network Science*														1					1	
61	*Leisure Studies*												1							1	
62	*Management Research News*							1												1	

63	*Management Research Review*															1				1	
64	*Organization Studies*																	1		1	
65	*Technological Fore-casting and Social Change*																		1	1	
66	*Tourism Planning and Development*																	1		1	
67	*Transformations in Business and Economics*															1				1	
	Total	1	0	0	1	3	2	2	1	7	6	3	8	7	11	12	19	43	40	166	

Asterisks indicate when a Journal has published a special issue on sustainable entrepreneurship

Business Strategy and the Environment (9 articles) were the most favorable outlets of publication in the field of sustainable entrepreneurship.

Tables 4.3 and 4.4 show the production and influence of authors, respectively. Table 4.3 shows the most prolific scholars in the field (i.e., authors with no less than three papers published) and the number of papers they authored or co-authored. Cohen and Muñoz seem to dominate the list. Indeed, Cohen B. and Muñoz P. co-authored several papers. However, the list of authors who have published one or two papers in the field of sustainable entrepreneurship is quite long; thus, it is worth concluding that the majority of authors in this study have not specialized in sustainable entrepreneurship but, rather, they have sparsely contributed to the growth of the field.

Table 4.4 outlines the most influential authors in the field, based on the citations received by each author. As can be seen in this table, the influence of an author derives from the importance that all other authors in the field attach to his/her work (i.e., the times an author is cited). Undoubtedly, Cohen B. stands out as the most important author in the field, as he embodies the most productive and the most-cited author.

Table 4.5 displays the ten most productive institutions in terms of sustainable entrepreneurship research in the last 17 years. These institutions are located in seven

Table 4.3 Top 10 contributing authors

Author	Papers
Cohen B	7
Muñoz P	7
Schaltegger S	6
Fichter K	5
Blok V	4
Lans T	4
Fellnhofer K	3
Hansen E G	3
Tiemann I	3
Wagner M	3

Table 4.4 Top 10 most influential authors

Author	Cites
Cohen B	83
Schaltegger S	81
Wagner M	78
Shepherd DA	76
Dean TJ	73
Patzelt H	71
McMullen JS	68
Winn MI	63
Venkataraman S	60
Hockerts K	54

Table 4.5 Top 10 research institutions

Institution	Papers	Country
Leuphana Universität Lüneburg	9	Germany
Wageningen University and Research Centre	7	Netherlands
Universität Oldenburg	6	Germany
University of Leeds	5	United Kingdom
Julius-Maximilians-Universität Würzburg	4	Germany
Lappeenrannan Teknillinen Yliopisto	4	Finland
Copenhagen Business School	4	Denmark
Ryerson University	4	Canada
EADA Business School	4	Spain
University of Liverpool Management School	4	United Kingdom

countries: three in Germany, two in the United Kingdom, and one in each of Canada, Denmark, Finland, the Netherlands, and Spain. The Leuphana Universität Lüneburg takes first place with nine articles, followed by the Wageningen University and Research Centre (7 articles), the Universität Oldenburg (6 articles), the University of Leeds (5 papers), and the remaining six institutions with 4 articles each. It should be noted that an author might represent different institutions in diverse stages/phases of their careers; which is the reason why inconsistencies are reported between contributing authors and institutions. For example, the most productive and influential author—Cohen B.—represents the EADA Business School in four papers while, in the other three, he represents other institutions.

4.1.3 Leading Papers

Table 4.6 outlines the three five most cited articles from 2002 to 2019, all of which received more than 400 citations. This analysis is relevant, due to the fact that the citation number shows the popularity and influence of each paper in the scientific community. However, it should be clarified that a paper published in an earlier period has a higher chance of having a larger number of citations than a paper published in a later period; thus, the variable C/Y was calculated. Taking into account this variable, the most influential paper was published by Schaltegger and Wagner (2011) in Business Strategy and the Environment, with 52.33 citations per year.

In absolute terms, the most cited paper was "*Toward a theory of sustainable entrepreneurship: Reducing environmental degradation through entrepreneurial action*" from Dean and McMullen (2007), published in the Journal of Business Venturing with 504 citations. This article builds on the environmental economic and entrepreneurship literatures to propose a theoretical model which considers entrepreneurship as the solution to seize profitable opportunities and solve environmental problems. Indeed, according to the environmental economic perspective, market

Table 4.6 Top 3 leading papers

Title	Authors	Journal	Cites	Year	C/Y
Toward a theory of sustainable entrepreneurship: Reducing environmental degradation through entrepreneurial action	Dean TJ McMullen JS	J of Business Venturing	504	2007	38.77
Market imperfections, opportunity and sustainable entrepreneurship	Cohen B Winn MI	J of Business Venturing	475	2007	36.54
Sustainable entrepreneurship and sustainability innovation: Categories and interactions	Schaltegger S Wagner M	Business Strategy and the Environment	471	2011	52.33

failures cause environmental degradation; similarly, the entrepreneurship literature argues that market failures inherently hold opportunities for achieving profitability.

The second most-cited article is "*Market imperfections, opportunity and sustainable entrepreneurship*", published by Cohen and Winn (2007) in the Journal of Business Venturing, with 475 citations. This paper examines four types of market imperfections (i.e., inefficient firms, externalities, flawed pricing mechanisms, and information asymmetries) which might offer significant business opportunities for sustainability-driven ventures. The paper suggests that the study of the relationship between market imperfections and entrepreneurial opportunities, and the emerging field of sustainable entrepreneurship are promising area for future studies.

The third most-cited paper was "*Sustainable entrepreneurship and sustainability innovation: categories and interactions*", published by Schaltegger and Wagner (2011) in Business Strategy and the Environment, with 471 citations. This article explains the conditions under which sustainable entrepreneurship (i.e., the application of the entrepreneurial approach to meet societal objectives while changing market contexts) and sustainability innovation emerge spontaneously, as well as which firms are most likely to step forward, in terms of sustainability innovation. The paper measures sustainable entrepreneurship and elaborates a classification matrix to assess the position of a firm in relation to its degree of environmental or social responsibility orientation. The sustainability orientation of the firm is evaluated by looking at its social and environmental goals and policies, management, and communication. Ultimately, the market impact of the firm is measured on the basis of market share, sales growth, and the reactions of competitors.

4.2 Scientific Mapping: Results from Network Analysis

As previously explained, bibliographic coupling links documents that reference the same set of cited documents (Boyack & Klavans, 2010). In this sense, Fig. 4.2 shows the map structure of coupled references produced by the Vos Viewer version 1.6 software (i.e., articles that were coupled at least five times; of the 166 original articles, 91 met the threshold). Further, as some items were not connected to each

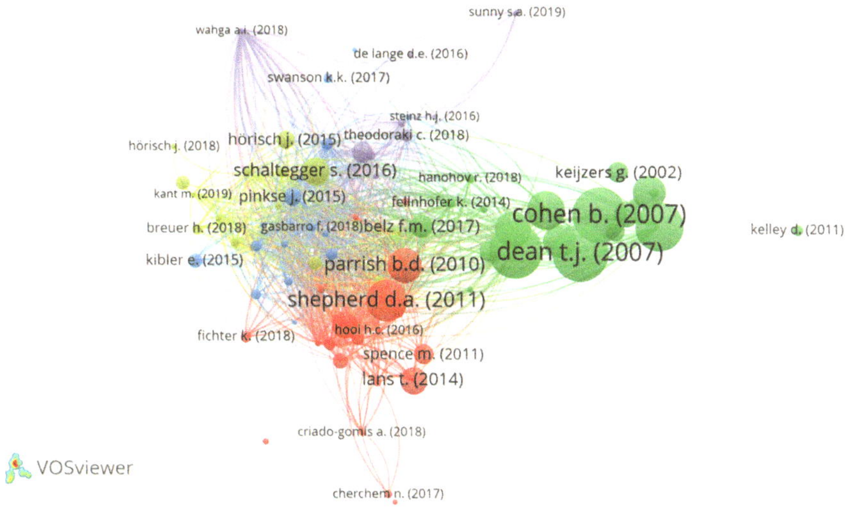

Fig. 4.2 Network map of articles in the sustainable entrepreneurship literature

other, the largest set of connected items consisted of 81 items. The association strength normalization was applied. The initial number of clusters was six; however, a preliminary qualitative assessment of clusters led the author to identify the final five clusters (Ardito, Scuotto, Del Giudice, & Petruzzelli, 2019).

The size and color of the nodes represent the number of references that are shared among the papers analyzed. The strength of a link indicates the number of cited references that two publications have in common. The presented map shows 81 nodes, 1861 links (total link strength: 5331), and five clusters.

4.2.1 The Cluster Identification

Identification of the five clusters enabled us to look at the structure of the literature in more depth, in order to gain additional insights into the current research interests and potential directions for future research (Fahimnia, Sarkis, & Davarzani, 2015). With this aim, Table 4.7 reports the total number of papers in each cluster, in size order: clusters 1 and 2 were the biggest (20 papers included), while cluster 5 was the smallest (11 papers included). These algorithmically identified clusters allowed us to classify the frontiers of sustainable entrepreneurship literature. Despite each cluster having its own clear specificities, it is interesting to note that clusters were linked by certain papers that acted as bridges.

After reading the paper abstracts, each of the five clusters was named after the common themes that linked the articles in each cluster (see Table 4.7). Then, one senior researcher, an expert in the field of social and sustainable entrepreneurship,

Table 4.7 The identified clusters of papers in the time span 2002–2019

Cluster	Number of articles in cluster	Thematic label
1	20	The sustainable Entrepreneur
2	20	Sources of opportunities for Sustainable Entrepreneurship
3	16	Sustainable businesses
4	14	Enabling factors of sustainable entrepreneurship in transition economies
5	11	Precursors to successful sustainable start-ups

was involved in the discussion of the assignment of category labels to each cluster, in order to identify a shared solution to name each cluster. Finally, the clusters were called:

1. The sustainable entrepreneur;
2. Sources of opportunities for sustainable entrepreneurship;
3. Sustainable businesses;
4. Enabling factors of sustainable entrepreneurship in transition economies;
5. Precursors to successful sustainable start-ups.

The volume moves now to detailing the content of the papers in each cluster from a qualitative perspective. As suggested by Ardito et al. (2019), the content of the lead papers in each cluster are presented in detail.

References

Ardito, L., Scuotto, V., Del Giudice, M., & Petruzzelli, A. M. (2019). A Bibliometric Analysis of Research on Big Data Analytics for Business and Management. *Management Decision, 57*(8), 1993–2009. https://doi.org/10.1108/MD-07-2018-0754

Boyack, K. W., & Klavans, R. (2010). Co-Citation Analysis, Bibliographic Coupling, and Direct Citation: Which Citation Approach Represents the Research Front Most Accurately? *Journal of the American Society for Information Science and Technology, 61*(12), 2389–2404. https://doi.org/10.1002/asi.21419

Cohen, B., & Winn, M. I. (2007). Market imperfections, opportunity and sustainable entrepreneurship. *Journal of Business Venturing, 22*(1), 29–49. Scopus. https://doi.org/10.1016/j.jbusvent.2004.12.001

Dean, T. J., & McMullen, J. S. (2007). Toward a theory of sustainable entrepreneurship: Reducing environmental degradation through entrepreneurial action. *Journal of Business Venturing, 22* (1), 50–76. Scopus. https://doi.org/10.1016/j.jbusvent.2005.09.003

Fahimnia, B., Sarkis, J., & Davarzani, H. (2015). Green Supply Chain Management: A Review and Bibliometric Analysis. *International Journal of Production Economics, 162*, 101–114. https://doi.org/10.1016/j.ijpe.2015.01.003

Schaltegger, S., & Wagner, M. (2011). Sustainable Entrepreneurship and Sustainability Innovation: Categories and Interactions. *Business Strategy and the Environment, 20*(4), 222–237. Scopus. https://doi.org/10.1002/bse.682

Chapter 5
Toward a Systematic Review of the Literature: Content Analysis

In the final step of the review process, the articles were qualitatively analyzed according to their content. Presumably due to its hybrid nature, sustainable entrepreneurship issues have been addressed in the literature from various perspectives, focusing on different aspects of the phenomenon.

Inspired by previous literature reviews on the topic, and after having read all the articles, the *purpose*, the *typology* (whether the paper was theoretical, empirical, or a literature review), the *methodology* (whether empirical papers relied on quantitative, qualitative, or mixed methodologies), the type of *analyses* performed (e.g., OLS regression, SEM), and the *findings* of each paper were accurately screened and assessed.

5.1 The Sustainable Entrepreneur

The first cluster included articles aimed at identifying the individual traits and characteristics (e.g., attitude and skills) that might boost or inhibit the intention to become a sustainable entrepreneur (i.e., the actor that starts the sustainable venture).

To date, studies in this sub-realm of research have identified knowledge and skills, self-efficacy, motivation and intention, values and attitudes, and business orientation as central explanatory variables in sustainable entrepreneurship (Muñoz & Cohen, 2018); for instance, in (Patzelt & Shepherd, 2011), the authors claimed that individuals differ one from another in their ability to recognize sustainability-related opportunities because of their prior knowledge of social and environmental settings, in relation to entrepreneurial values and motives. Similarly, Spence, Ben Boubaker Gherib, and Biwolé (2011) underlined the importance of the individual values of entrepreneurs to engage in sustainable venturing, even if socio-cultural and institutional peculiarities might have stronger (weaker) impacts on the adoption of sustainable practices. Given the importance of values —especially

M. Pinna, *Sustainable Entrepreneurship*, SpringerBriefs in Business,
https://doi.org/10.1007/978-3-030-57818-3_5

pro-environmental ones— individual moral cognition and competencies have emerged as crucial indicators of the ability to actively pursue opportunities for sustainable development (Ploum, Blok, Lans, & Omta, 2018). To the contrary, Shepherd, Patzelt, and Baron (2013) strongly argued the case for the influence of moral disengagement in shaping the ability to recognize sustainability opportunities of entrepreneurs and their willingness to actively run a sustainable enterprise. Aside from these morally relevant antecedents, the creation of new sustainable ventures has been found to be influenced by one's sustainability orientation (Wagner, 2012), entrepreneurial orientation (Cherchem, 2017; Criado-Gomis, Iniesta-Bonillo, & Cervera-Taulet, 2018), and entrepreneurial bricolage (Hooi, Ahmad, Amran, & Rahman, 2016).

Interestingly, a few of the papers in this cluster maintained the importance of education as a system supporting sustainability-oriented entrepreneurship (e.g., Cincera et al., 2018). In fact, higher education institutions are the ideal environment to prepare the mindset of future sustainable entrepreneurs (Fichter & Tiemann, 2018). Indeed, Universities have been appointed as capable of developing specific competencies (e.g., sustainable development competence, systems thinking competence, embracing diversity and interdisciplinarity, and foresighted thinking) which enhance sustainable entrepreneurship among students (Lans, Blok, & Wesselink, 2014). In a similar vein, Biberhofer, Lintner, Bernhardt, and Rieckmann (2019) found that Universities should adopt an action-oriented process view that empowers future entrepreneurs by developing their knowledge of values and worldviews, competencies, and opportunities to boost their future work performance.

5.2 Source of Opportunities for Sustainable Entrepreneurship

Papers in the second cluster focused on the foundation of the concept of sustainable entrepreneurship. More specifically, sustainable entrepreneurship is understood as a new field of study that bridges entrepreneurship theory and sustainable development. To this extent, the articles in this cluster are mainly conceptual and try to advance the knowledge on sustainable entrepreneurship by proposing new interpretive models and applying them to single case studies. In this vein, authors have attempted to highlight the relevance of sustainable entrepreneurship as a new independent field of research, both for theory and practice. For instance, Dean and McMullen (2007) articulated the domain of sustainable entrepreneurship by explaining how entrepreneurship can help to solve environmental problems in global socio-economic systems. Similarly, entrepreneurship can contribute to solving environmental problems through helping extant institutions in achieving their goals and by creating new, more environmentally sustainable products, services, and institutions (York & Venkataraman, 2010).

Earlier contributions have tried to explain which conditions would be necessary to promote the actual shift of firms to sustainable development in a long-term perspective; for example, Keijzers (2002) defined the major strategies (e.g., a systematic investigation of the ecological and business horizon of the firm and a systematic strategic investigation of the sources of potential value creation) to overcome the factors that inhibit the shift to sustainability. Other contributions have identified the market imperfections that have contributed to environmental degradation, assessed their importance as entrepreneurial opportunities, and suggested a model of sustainable entrepreneurship (Cohen & Winn, 2007). Further, the transition to a sustainable economy is enhanced by the presence of new sustainable ventures, thanks to their ability find innovative social and environmental solutions (Hockerts & Wüstenhagen, 2010; Schaltegger & Wagner, 2011).

More recent contributions have identified new ways to enhance the transition to sustainability. For instance, Zeng (2018) argued that new technologies (i.e., big data internet systems) can foster future sustainable growth with better action to environmental and social problems, while Hanohov and Baldacchino (2018) provide qualitative evidence of the importance of knowledge (e.g., natural, communal, or entrepreneurial) to properly recognize sustainability opportunities. Finally, Anbarasan and Sushil (2018) claimed that an increase in shareholder value and taking into account the needs of employee benefits must be considered as a determinant or enabler of sustainability.

5.3 Sustainable Businesses

The third cluster is comprised of articles that basically discussed the importance of adapting sustainable strategies to diverse scenarios. More specifically, the first sub-group of papers postulates that diverse industries (e.g., clean energy sector, tourism) need different solutions to get the best out of sustainable opportunities in the market (Pinkse & Groot, 2015; Swanson & DeVereaux, 2017); for instance, in the tourism sector, it is important to "adapt entrepreneurial models that sustain and enhance the values and traditions of a community for its self-defined benefits, rather than imposing economic entrepreneurial models that may change conditions within a community" (Swanson & DeVereaux, 2017, p. 78). Similarly, the second group of papers focuses on how sustainable strategies and business models have to be harmonized in diverse countries, especially developing ones (e.g., Maas, Bunders, & Zweekhorst, 2015; Meis Mason, Dana, & Anderson, 2012); for example, Gray, Duncan, Kirkwood, and Walton (2014) showed that key specific organizational capabilities are necessary for coping with exogenous shocks in South Pacific island states. Indeed, specific situations require likewise specific solutions.

5.4 Enabling Factors of Sustainable Entrepreneurship in Transition Economies

The articles in the fourth cluster elaborated on the factors which facilitate the transition towards more sustainable economies (e.g., transitioning to low carbon energy solutions). The first group of papers in this cluster pinpoint sustainability-driven business models (i.e., hybrid business models which are able to reconcile economic, social, and environmental goals) as a critical factor which ensures a factual transition towards sustainability (Breuer, Fichter, Lüdeke-Freund, & Tiemann, 2018; Hahn, Spieth, & Ince, 2018; Hansen & Schaltegger, 2013; Hörisch, 2015; Schaltegger, Lüdeke-Freund, & Hansen, 2016). These papers generally rely on single or multiple case studies to provide evidence for their hypotheses. As the development of sustainable business models is a complex process which requires a supportive entrepreneurial ecosystem (Neumeyer & Santos, 2018), the second group of contributions argued for the importance for sustainable entrepreneurs and ventures to engage with institutional (i.e., educational institutions) and public (i.e., regional political actors) authorities, in order to facilitate the transition from traditional businesses towards more sustainable ones. The authors in this second group mostly employed case studies and structured or semi-structured interviews (Gasbarro, Annunziata, Rizzi, & Frey, 2017; Silajdžić, Kurtagić, & Vučijak, 2015; Tiemann, Fichter, & Geier, 2018). Finally, a third group of studies discussed the importance of innovation as the most important ingredient to promote the success of the sustainability formula. (Davies & Chambers, 2018; Kant & Kanda, 2019; Klewitz, 2017). Innovation has been interpreted both as a factor that needs to be integrated within sustainable business models, or as an actor (i.e., innovation intermediaries) to enable the transition process towards sustainability.

5.5 Precursors to Successful Sustainable Start-Ups

The studies in the fifth cluster focused on sustainable start-ups. In particular, the strategies that facilitate or hinder the successful development of start-ups were investigated with qualitative methodologies (i.e., case studies and semi-structured interviews were mostly employed, and thematic analyses were generally performed, except for three papers which relied on regression analyses, such as OLS and negative binomial). One group of these studies provided empirical evidence on the importance of external investments and venture capital for the successful development of start-ups (Bocken, 2015; de Lange, 2016, 2017). The second group delved into how local and geographic factors contribute to the entrepreneurial growth of sustainable new ventures or start-ups (Giudici, Guerini, & Rossi-Lamastra, 2019; Griffiths, Gundry, Kickul, & Muñoz Fernandez, 2009; Sunny & Shu, 2019). Finally, a couple articles pinpointed the importance of backing organizations, such as business incubators, to support start-ups towards sustainability (Bank & Kanda, 2016; Theodoraki, Messeghem, & Rice, 2018).

References

Anbarasan, P., & Sushil, P. (2018). Stakeholder Engagement in Sustainable Enterprise: Evolving a Conceptual Framework, and a Case Study of ITC. *Business Strategy and the Environment, 27* (3), 282–299. Scopus. https://doi.org/10.1002/bse.1999

Bank, N., & Kanda, W. (2016). Tenant Recruitment and Support Processes in Sustainability-Profiled Business Incubators. *Industry and Higher Education, 30*(4), 267–277. Scopus. https://doi.org/10.1177/0950422216659567

Biberhofer, P., Lintner, C., Bernhardt, J., & Rieckmann, M. (2019). Facilitating Work Performance of Sustainability-Driven Entrepreneurs Through Higher Education: The Relevance of Competencies, Values, Worldviews and Opportunities. *International Journal of Entrepreneurship and Innovation, 20*(1), 21–38. Scopus. https://doi.org/10.1177/1465750318755881

Bocken, N. M. P. (2015). Sustainable Venture Capital—Catalyst for Sustainable Start-Up Success? *Journal of Cleaner Production, 108*, 647–658. Scopus. https://doi.org/10.1016/j.jclepro.2015.05.079

Breuer, H., Fichter, K., Lüdeke-Freund, F., & Tiemann, I. (2018). Sustainability-Oriented Business Model Development: Principles, Criteria and Tools. *International Journal of Entrepreneurial Venturing, 10*(2), 256–286. Scopus. https://doi.org/10.1504/IJEV.2018.092715

Cherchem, N. (2017). The Relationship Between Organizational Culture and Entrepreneurial Orientation in Family Firms: Does Generational Involvement Matter? *Journal of Family Business Strategy, 8*(2), 87–98. Scopus. https://doi.org/10.1016/j.jfbs.2017.04.001

Cincera, J., Biberhofer, P., Binka, B., Boman, J., Mindt, L., & Rieckmann, M. (2018). Designing a Sustainability-Driven Entrepreneurship Curriculum as a Social Learning Process: A Case Study from an International Knowledge Alliance Project. *Journal of Cleaner Production, 172*, 4357–4366. Scopus. https://doi.org/10.1016/j.jclepro.2017.05.051

Cohen, B., & Winn, M. I. (2007). Market Imperfections, Opportunity and Sustainable Entrepreneurship. *Journal of Business Venturing, 22*(1), 29–49. Scopus. https://doi.org/10.1016/j.jbusvent.2004.12.001

Criado-Gomis, A., Iniesta-Bonillo, M., & Cervera-Taulet, A. (2018). Sustainable Entrepreneurial Orientation Within an Intrapreneurial Context: Effects on Business Performance. *International Entrepreneurship and Management Journal, 14*(2), 295–308. Scopus. https://doi.org/10.1007/s11365-018-0503-x

Davies, I. A., & Chambers, L. (2018). Integrating Hybridity and Business Model Theory in Sustainable Entrepreneurship. *Journal of Cleaner Production, 177*, 378–386. Scopus. https://doi.org/10.1016/j.jclepro.2017.12.196

de Lange, D. E. (2016). A Social Capital Paradox: Entrepreneurial Dynamism in a Small World Clean Technology Cluster. *Journal of Cleaner Production, 139*, 576–585. Scopus. https://doi.org/10.1016/j.jclepro.2016.08.080

de Lange, D. E. (2017). Start-Up Sustainability: An Insurmountable Cost or a Life-Giving Investment? *Journal of Cleaner Production, 156*, 838–854. Scopus. https://doi.org/10.1016/j.jclepro.2017.04.108

Dean, T. J., & McMullen, J. S. (2007). Toward a theory of sustainable entrepreneurship: Reducing environmental degradation through entrepreneurial action. *Journal of Business Venturing, 22* (1), 50–76. Scopus. https://doi.org/10.1016/j.jbusvent.2005.09.003

Fichter, K., & Tiemann, I. (2018). Factors Influencing University Support for Sustainable Entrepreneurship: Insights from Explorative Case Studies. *Journal of Cleaner Production, 175*, 512–524. Scopus. https://doi.org/10.1016/j.jclepro.2017.12.031

Gasbarro, F., Annunziata, E., Rizzi, F., & Frey, M. (2017). The Interplay Between Sustainable Entrepreneurs and Public Authorities: Evidence From Sustainable Energy Transitions. *Organization and Environment, 30*(3), 226–252. Scopus. https://doi.org/10.1177/1086026616669211

Giudici, G., Guerini, M., & Rossi-Lamastra, C. (2019). The Creation of Cleantech Startups at the Local Level: The Role of Knowledge Availability and Environmental Awareness. *Small Business Economics, 52*(4), 815–830. Scopus. https://doi.org/10.1007/s11187-017-9936-9

Gray, B. J., Duncan, S., Kirkwood, J., & Walton, S. (2014). Encouraging Sustainable Entrepreneurship in Climate-Threatened Communities: A Samoan Case Study. *Entrepreneurship and Regional Development, 26*(5–6), 401–430. Scopus. https://doi.org/10.1080/08985626.2014.922622

Griffiths, M. D., Gundry, L., Kickul, J., & Muñoz Fernandez, A. (2009). Innovation Ecology as a Precursor to Entrepreneurial Growth: A Cross/Country Empirical Investigation. *Journal of Small Business and Enterprise Development, 16*(3), 375–390. Scopus. https://doi.org/10.1108/14626000910977116

Hahn, R., Spieth, P., & Ince, I. (2018). Business Model Design in Sustainable Entrepreneurship: Illuminating the Commercial Logic of Hybrid Businesses. *Journal of Cleaner Production, 176*, 439–451. Scopus. https://doi.org/10.1016/j.jclepro.2017.12.167

Hanohov, R., & Baldacchino, L. (2018). Opportunity Recognition in Sustainable Entrepreneurship: An Exploratory Study. *International Journal of Entrepreneurial Behaviour and Research, 24*(2), 333–358. Scopus. https://doi.org/10.1108/IJEBR-12-2015-0275

Hansen, E. G., & Schaltegger, S. (2013). 100 Per Cent Organic? A Sustainable Entrepreneurship Perspective on the Diffusion of Organic Clothing. *Corporate Governance (Bingley), 13*(5), 583–598. Scopus. https://doi.org/10.1108/CG-06-2013-0074

Hockerts, K., & Wüstenhagen, R. (2010). Greening Goliaths Versus Emerging Davids—Theorizing About the Role of Incumbents and New Entrants in Sustainable Entrepreneurship. *Journal of Business Venturing, 25*(5), 481–492. https://doi.org/10.1016/j.jbusvent.2009.07.005

Hooi, H. C., Ahmad, N. H., Amran, A., & Rahman, S. A. (2016). The Functional Role of Entrepreneurial Orientation and Entrepreneurial Bricolage in Ensuring Sustainable Entrepreneurship. *Management Research Review, 39*(12), 1616–1638. Scopus. https://doi.org/10.1108/MRR-06-2015-0144

Hörisch, J. (2015). Crowdfunding for Environmental Ventures: An Empirical Analysis of the Influence of Environmental Orientation on the Success of Crowdfunding Initiatives. *Journal of Cleaner Production, 107*, 636–645. Scopus. https://doi.org/10.1016/j.jclepro.2015.05.046

Kant, M., & Kanda, W. (2019). Innovation Intermediaries: What Does It Take to Survive Over Time? *Journal of Cleaner Production, 229*, 911–930. Scopus. https://doi.org/10.1016/j.jclepro.2019.04.213

Keijzers, G. (2002). The Transition to the Sustainable Enterprise. *Journal of Cleaner Production, 10*(4), 349–359. Scopus. https://doi.org/10.1016/S0959-6526(01)00051-8

Klewitz, J. (2017). Grazing, Exploring and Networking for Sustainability-Oriented Innovations in Learning-Action Networks: An SME Perspective. *Innovation, 30*(4), 476–503. Scopus. https://doi.org/10.1080/13511610.2015.1070090

Lans, T., Blok, V., & Wesselink, R. (2014). Learning Apart and Together: Towards an Integrated Competence Framework for Sustainable Entrepreneurship in Higher Education. *Journal of Cleaner Production, 62*, 37–47. Scopus. https://doi.org/10.1016/j.jclepro.2013.03.036

Maas, J., Bunders, J. F. G., & Zweekhorst, M. B. M. (2015). Trust Building and Entrepreneurial Behaviour in a Distrusting Environment: A Longitudinal Study from Bangladesh. *International Journal of Business and Globalisation, 14*(1), 75–96. Scopus. https://doi.org/10.1504/IJBG.2015.066100

Meis Mason, A. H., Dana, L.-P., & Anderson, R. B. (2012). Getting Ready for Oil and Gas Development in Canada's Northwest Territories: Aboriginal Entrepreneurship and Economic Development. *International Journal of Entrepreneurship and Small Business, 16*(3), 242–266. Scopus. https://doi.org/10.1504/12.47434

Muñoz, P., & Cohen, B. (2018). Sustainable Entrepreneurship Research: Taking Stock and Looking Ahead. *Business Strategy and the Environment, 27*(3), 300–322. Scopus. https://doi.org/10.1002/bse.2000

Neumeyer, X., & Santos, S. C. (2018). Sustainable Business Models, Venture Typologies, and Entrepreneurial Ecosystems: A Social Network Perspective. *Journal of Cleaner Production, 172*, 4565–4579. Scopus. https://doi.org/10.1016/j.jclepro.2017.08.216

Patzelt, H., & Shepherd, D. A. (2011). Recognizing Opportunities for Sustainable Development. *Entrepreneurship Theory and Practice, 35*(4), 631–652. https://doi.org/10.1111/j.1540-6520.2010.00386.x

Pinkse, J., & Groot, K. (2015). Sustainable Entrepreneurship and Corporate Political Activity: Overcoming Market Barriers in The Clean Energy Sector. *Entrepreneurship: Theory and Practice, 39*(3), 633–654. Scopus. https://doi.org/10.1111/etap.12055

Ploum, L., Blok, V., Lans, T., & Omta, O. (2018). Exploring the Relation Between Individual Moral Antecedents and Entrepreneurial Opportunity Recognition for Sustainable Development. *Journal of Cleaner Production, 172*, 1582–1591. Scopus. https://doi.org/10.1016/j.jclepro.2017.10.296

Schaltegger, S., Lüdeke-Freund, F., & Hansen, E. G. (2016). Business Models for Sustainability: A Co-Evolutionary Analysis of Sustainable Entrepreneurship, Innovation, and Transformation. *Organization and Environment, 29*(3), 264–289. Scopus. https://doi.org/10.1177/1086026616633272

Schaltegger, S., & Wagner, M. (2011). Sustainable Entrepreneurship and Sustainability Innovation: Categories and Interactions. *Business Strategy and the Environment, 20*(4), 222–237. Scopus. https://doi.org/10.1002/bse.682

Shepherd, D. A., Patzelt, H., & Baron, R. A. (2013). I Care About Nature, But. Disengaging Values in Assessing Opportunities That Cause Harm. *Academy of Management Journal, 56*(5), 1251–1273. Scopus. https://doi.org/10.5465/amj.2011.0776

Silajdžić, I., Kurtagić, S. M., & Vučijak, B. (2015). Green Entrepreneurship in Transition Economies: A Case Study of Bosnia and Herzegovina. *Journal of Cleaner Production, 88*, 376–384. Scopus. https://doi.org/10.1016/j.jclepro.2014.07.004

Spence, M., Ben Boubaker Gherib, J., & Biwolé, V. O. (2011). Sustainable Entrepreneurship: Is Entrepreneurial Will Enough? A North-South Comparison. *Journal of Business Ethics, 99*(3), 335–367. Scopus. https://doi.org/10.1007/s10551-010-0656-1

Sunny, S. A., & Shu, C. (2019). Investments, Incentives, and Innovation: Geographical Clustering Dynamics as Drivers of Sustainable Entrepreneurship. *Small Business Economics, 52*(4), 905–927. Scopus. https://doi.org/10.1007/s11187-017-9941-z

Swanson, K. K., & DeVereaux, C. (2017). A Theoretical Framework for Sustaining Culture: Culturally Sustainable Entrepreneurship. *Annals of Tourism Research, 62*, 78–88. Scopus. https://doi.org/10.1016/j.annals.2016.12.003

Theodoraki, C., Messeghem, K., & Rice, M. P. (2018). A Social Capital Approach to the Development of Sustainable Entrepreneurial Ecosystems: An Explorative Study. *Small Business Economics, 51*(1), 153–170. Scopus. https://doi.org/10.1007/s11187-017-9924-0

Tiemann, I., Fichter, K., & Geier, J. (2018). University Support Systems for Sustainable Entrepreneurship: Insights from Explorative Case Studies. *International Journal of Entrepreneurial Venturing, 10*(1), 83–110. Scopus. https://doi.org/10.1504/IJEV.2018.090990

Wagner, M. (2012). Ventures for the Public Good and Entrepreneurial Intentions: An Empirical Analysis of Sustainability Orientation as a Determining Factor. *Journal of Small Business and Entrepreneurship, 25*(4), 519–531. Scopus. https://doi.org/10.1080/08276331.2012.10593587

York, J. G., & Venkataraman, S. (2010). The Entrepreneur–Environment Nexus: Uncertainty, Innovation, and Allocation. *Journal of Business Venturing, 25*(5), 449–463. https://doi.org/10.1016/j.jbusvent.2009.07.007

Zeng, J. (2018). Fostering Path of Ecological Sustainable Entrepreneurship Within Big Data Network System. *International Entrepreneurship and Management Journal, 14*(1), 79–95. Scopus. https://doi.org/10.1007/s11365-017-0466-3

Chapter 6
Discussion, Managerial Implications, and Future Steps

The bibliometric and content analyses which were carried out allow us to systematically review the research field of sustainable entrepreneurship. However, diverse methodologies lead to diverse insights. To this extent, this chapter argues what has been achieved in the literature and suggests further steps for researchers and practitioners.

6.1 Insights from Bibliometric Analysis

The bibliometric analyses unveiled the main trends in sustainable research by looking at the evolution in the number of published articles, the most influential journals and papers, and the most prolific authors, institutions, and countries.

Looking at the publishing chronological trend, the field of sustainable entrepreneurship is still in its infancy: the first paper dates back to 2002, but the largest amount of articles has been published only recently (i.e., +75% from 2015 to 2019). Further, 10 journals have hosted 92 out of 166 articles, with the Journal of Cleaner Production, the Journal of Business Venturing, and Business Strategy and the Environment being the most favorable outlets of publication. In terms of authorship, the majority of researchers in this area have not specialized in sustainable entrepreneurship; rather, they have sparsely contributed to the growth of the field. However, it is worth mentioning that Boyd Cohen is the most prolific and influential scholar in the field. Remarkably, research on sustainable entrepreneurship is definitely a European and North American business (see Table 4.6); therefore, new studies are especially needed from Asian and South American countries, both for scientific advances and to provide viable business solutions in these communities.

From a practical point of view, the findings from the bibliometric analyses herein can be useful for authors entering sustainable entrepreneurship as a new research

M. Pinna, *Sustainable Entrepreneurship*, SpringerBriefs in Business,
https://doi.org/10.1007/978-3-030-57818-3_6

field and might serve as a theoretical introduction to the field for students and managers.

6.2 Insights from Content Analysis

The content analysis revealed that the majority of published articles in the field of sustainable entrepreneurship—especially the earliest ones—were theoretical or reported results of case study research, which is not surprising, given the emerging character of the field. As a first suggestion, the author claims that the discussion on sustainable entrepreneurship should benefit from shifting from qualitative to quantitative methodologies, thus retrieving larger-scale data (both primary and secondary), adopting different research designs (i.e., experiments), and implementing additional analyses (e.g., SEM analyses, among others).

Looking more deeply at the literature, studies on sustainable entrepreneurship seem to have converged upon five clusters, representing as many thematic categories. Compared to all other categories, the two most investigated topics were related to the "sustainable entrepreneur" theme (20 articles) and the "sources of opportunities for sustainable development" theme (20 papers), followed by the category "sustainable businesses" (16 papers).

Undoubtedly, the role of sustainable entrepreneurs in pursuing sustainable opportunities is at stake. Researchers, thus far, have identified several drivers of decision-making in sustainable entrepreneurs, sometimes overweighing the positive influence of individual traits (e.g., personality, values, socio-demographics) to the detriment of factors that might disengage entrepreneurs in the pursuit of sustainable business opportunities (except for Shepherd, Patzelt, & Baron, 2013). For this reason, experimental study designs that take into account *positive and negative factors that influence the individual's intention to create a sustainable venture* should be further investigated in the future.

Moreover, the category "sources of opportunities for sustainable development" pinpoints market imperfections as the most favorable condition that triggers sustainable entrepreneurship. However, *how to recognize and achieve business opportunities* that harmonize economic, social, and environmental goals is the greatest challenge in sustainable entrepreneurship, which should be increasingly addressed in future studies.

In particular, the "sustainable businesses" category focused on how sustainable business practices have been differently applied, according to the industry and country in which they are implemented. Within this category, specific attention has been paid to the completion of sustainable solutions by firms operating in cleantech industries and developing countries, mostly relying on single or multiple case studies. Future contributions could attempt to *develop and validate a generalizable model of sustainable entrepreneurship* that has the potential to be applied across a considerable number of industries and countries (both developed and developing) which are representative of the phenomenon.

The remaining categories took into account two additional themes which have encountered slightly less interest from the scientific community; namely, the category "enabling factors of sustainable entrepreneurship in transition economies" (14 papers) and the "precursors to successful sustainable start-ups" theme (11 articles).

Aside from the role of entrepreneurs as facilitators of sustainable development, sustainable business models and educational institutions are important enablers of the transition to sustainable ventures. The existing literature has suggested that the identification and development of sustainable business models is part of a firm's innovative business strategy. Innovation appears as the key component in the exploitation of new sustainable opportunities, a core element in supportive entrepreneurial ecosystems, and a crucial topic in academic curricula. In this context, a prompt understanding of *which specific knowledge* (i.e., whether entrepreneurial or sustainability focused) is actually needed to develop innovative but viable sustainable solutions, and *how public institutions* (both governmental and educational ones) *can effectively become supportive entrepreneurial ecosystems and how the relationship between firms and institutions in the ecosystem should actually unfold in order to maximize the firm's sustainability outcome*.

Finally, another theme that has attracted scholarly attention is related to the analysis of the "precursors to successful sustainable start-ups". Among such antecedents, the literature has pinpointed investments and business incubators as factors that have the potential to accelerate or hinder the successful implementation of sustainable start-ups. Additional efforts must be undertaken in the direction of *understanding how business incubators can support sustainable start-ups in the process of improving their value proposition in a way that helps them attract the best investors*.

With regard to the managerial implications of this volume, the content analysis findings might help future entrepreneurs to understand the importance of recognizing sustainable business opportunities and how to develop feasible business models that encounter the appreciation of venture capitalists and investors, thus obtaining substantial funding to start a new sustainable venture. Actual entrepreneurs may also benefit from the results of this review by gaining insights into the transition from traditional business models to more sustainable ones, adapting it to the specific features of their market, industry, or country. Further, given the importance of supportive ecosystems for the creation and development of new sustainable ventures, the results of this review might help business incubator managers to quickly identify which papers to read, in order to build a real supportive environment. Similarly, our findings might help university managers to raise awareness on the specific knowledge that is needed to ensure current students have access to the most appropriate information and skills to start a sustainable venture.

Reference

Shepherd, D. A., Patzelt, H., & Baron, R. A. (2013). I Care About Nature, But. Disengaging Values in Assessing Opportunities That Cause Harm. *Academy of Management Journal, 56*(5), 1251–1273. Scopus. https://doi.org/10.5465/amj.2011.0776

Chapter 7
Conclusion

This volume has presented a systematic review of the field of sustainable entrepreneurship, thus falling into the broader goal of review studies. More specifically, the main objective of this volume was to scrutinize, classify, and systematize the streams of literature published between 2002 and 2019 that lie at the intersection of the entrepreneurship and sustainability realms. For the purposes of this volume, an objective approach has been adopted: that is, bibliometric performance indicators and scientific mapping analyses have been completed. Then, a subjective approach was performed; that is, qualitative evaluation of the clusters was performed by looking at the content of the papers included in each cluster of the scientific map. By taking advantage of the complementing capacity of both the objective and subjective approaches, the volume offers a comprehensive understanding and a systematic assessment of the research in sustainable entrepreneurship. Despite having adopted a rigorous approach which helps to overcome the limits engrained in both objective and subjective methodologies (i.e., the personal judgments typically related to qualitative reviews), this book is not without limitations, suggesting challenges and guidelines for further development.

First, the research design of this volume relied on the Scopus database as its unique data source. Indeed, even if Scopus is the broadest abstract and citation collection of peer-reviewed scientific documents across all research fields, the data collection could be enriched by looking additionally, for example, at the Google Scholar database. Furthermore, our data belonged to a single thematic category—"Business, Management and Accounting"—which could have biased the generalization of our results. Future reviews could consider including articles from diverse disciplinary areas, in order to understand whether this solution could provide a more complete overview of the phenomenon.

Second, despite bibliometrics being one of the most objective approaches to literature reviews, it cannot account comprehensively for the complex nature of the citing behavior of authors (e.g., self-citations or self-legitimization strategies) (Vogel & Güttel, 2013). More specifically, in relation to the bibliometric

M. Pinna, *Sustainable Entrepreneurship*, SpringerBriefs in Business,
https://doi.org/10.1007/978-3-030-57818-3_7

performance indicator technique, this review focused on scholarly journal articles and has neglected to include other types of scientific documents, such as books, book chapters, and conference proceedings. Further, with reference to the scientific mapping technique, bibliographic coupling was selected as the most suitable methodology to detect topical areas of research in a scientific field (i.e. sustainable entrepreneurship) characterized by a young and vibrant scholarly publication production (Vogel & Güttel, 2013). However, as previously stated (see Fig. 3.2), bibliographic coupling overemphasizes publications with comparatively longer reference lists: the longer a bibliography is, the more likely it is to overlap with the reference lists of other publications. As a consequence, researchers should be aware of the peculiarities of this methodology and complement it with different bibliometric methods such as, for instance, co-citation analyses (see Terán-Yépez, Marín-Carrillo, del Pilar Casado-Belmonte, & de las Mercedes Capobianco-Uriarte, 2020).

Third, this review has strived to complement the bibliometric results with a qualitative assessment of the research production of sustainable entrepreneurship through content analysis. To this extent, the findings showed a strong prevalence of theoretical contributions in the second cluster, whereas empirical papers were quite widespread in the remaining clusters. From a methodological standpoint, it is worth mentioning that a vast majority of empirical papers rely on qualitative methods, especially case studies or interviews, which are thematically/content analyzed. On the other hand, very few articles have adopted quantitative methodologies to provide evidence on sustainable entrepreneurship; on average, quantitative articles were analyzed through regression analyses (e.g., OLS and negative binomial regression). Therefore, although it is not surprising that a young research field has adopted qualitative methodologies to investigate a new phenomenon, future studies could provide additional quantitative empirical evidence by both collecting data from primary or secondary sources and performing additional analyses, such as structural equation modeling. In order to advance sustainable entrepreneurship research, there exists a need to "not only address issues related to boundary definitions, but also further substantive work [. . .] that provides a strong basis upon which we can build valid and reliable foundations for the field" (Doherty, Haugh, & Lyon, 2014, p. 324).

Finally, despite the fact that sustainable entrepreneurship has received considerable and increasing interest from academics, practitioners, and institutions over the last 10 years, there remains substantial room for further academic inquiry. Indeed, what is currently missing in the sustainable entrepreneurship literature ranges from how to recognize and achieve business opportunities that harmonize economic, social, and environmental goals to analyzing the positive and negative factors that can influence an individual's intention to create a sustainable venture; from identifying what *specific knowledge* (whether entrepreneurial or sustainability focused) entrepreneurs actually need to how public institutions (both governmental and educational ones) can effectively become supportive entrepreneurial ecosystems for future and actual entrepreneurs; and from developing and validating a generalizable model of sustainable entrepreneurship that has the potential to be applied across a considerable number of industries and countries (both developed and developing) to how business incubators can support sustainable start-ups in the process of improving their value propositions in a way that helps them to attract the best investors.

In conclusion, this volume has offered (hopefully) suggestive insights through the results of the bibliometric and content analyses performed. However, academic research on sustainable entrepreneurship keeps on gaining momentum across a growing range of disciplines and sectors (e.g., Sarango-Lalangui, Santos, & Hormiga, 2018), thus calling for periodic assessments of the field, in order to highlight its progress and limitations, to stimulate reflections on future research, and to motivate further attempts (e.g., Terán-Yépez et al., 2020). For instance, future studies could attain additional insights on sustainable entrepreneurship research by implementing a meta-analysis.

References

Doherty, B., Haugh, H., & Lyon, F. (2014). Social Enterprises as Hybrid Organizations: A Review and Research Agenda. *International Journal of Management Reviews, 16*(4), 417–436. https://doi.org/10.1111/ijmr.12028.

Sarango-Lalangui, P., Santos, J., & Hormiga, E. (2018). The Development of Sustainable Entrepreneurship Research Field. *Sustainability, 10*(6), 2005. https://doi.org/10.3390/su10062005

Terán-Yépez, E., Marín-Carrillo, G. M., del Pilar Casado-Belmonte, M., & de las Mercedes Capobianco-Uriarte, M. (2020). Sustainable Entrepreneurship: Review of Its Evolution and New Trends. *Journal of Cleaner Production, 252*, 119742. https://doi.org/10.1016/j.jclepro.2019.119742

Vogel, R., & Güttel, W. H. (2013). The Dynamic Capability View in Strategic Management: A Bibliometric Review: DCV in Strategic Management. *International Journal of Management Reviews, 15*, 426–446. https://doi.org/10.1111/ijmr.12000

Appendix

The list of articles included in the study

Authors	Year	Journal
G. Keijzers	2002	Journal of Cleaner Production
M. Lordkipanidze, H. Brezet, M. Backman	2005	Journal of Cleaner Production
B. Cohen	2006	Business Strategy and the Environment
W. Young, F. Tilley	2006	Business Strategy and the Environment
F. Tilley, B.D. Parrish	2006	World Review of Entrepreneurship, Management and Sustainable Development
T.J. Dean, J.S. McMullen	2007	Journal of Business Venturing
B. Cohen, M.I. Winn	2007	Journal of Business Venturing
B. Cohen, B. Smith, R. Mitchell	2008	Business Strategy and the Environment
D.Y. Choi, E.R. Gray	2008	Management Research News
M.D. Griffiths, L. Gundry, J. Kickul, A. Muñoz Fernandez	2009	Journal of Small Business and Enterprise Development
K. Hockerts, R. Wüstenhagen	2010	Journal of Business Venturing
J.G. York, S. Venkataraman	2010	Journal of Business Venturing
A. Kuckertz, M. Wagner	2010	Journal of Business Venturing
B.D. Parrish	2010	Journal of Business Venturing
D.F. Pacheco, T.J. Dean, D.S. Payne	2010	Journal of Business Venturing
C. Rodgers	2010	Corporate Social Responsibility and Environmental Management
R. De Palma, V. Dobes	2010	Journal of Cleaner Production
S. Schaltegger, M. Wagner	2011	Business Strategy and the Environment
D.A. Shepherd, H. Patzelt	2011	Entrepreneurship: Theory and Practice
M. Spence, J. Ben Boubaker Gherib, V.O. Biwolé	2011	Journal of Business Ethics
D. Kelley	2011	Business Horizons

(continued)

M. Pinna, *Sustainable Entrepreneurship*, SpringerBriefs in Business,
https://doi.org/10.1007/978-3-030-57818-3

Authors	Year	Journal
M. Wagner	2011	International Journal of Entrepreneurship and Small Business
J.-J. Obrecht	2011	International Journal of Entrepreneurship and Small Business
M. Wagner	2012	Journal of Small Business and Entrepreneurship
K.K. Swanson, C. DeVereaux	2012	Advances in Culture, Tourism and Hospitality Research
A.H. Meis Mason, L.-P. Dana, R.B. Anderson	2012	International Journal of Entrepreneurship and Small Business
D.A. Shepherd, H. Patzelt, R.A. Baron	2013	Academy of Management Journal
D. Keskin, J.C. Diehl, N. Molenaar	2013	Journal of Cleaner Production
E.G. Hansen, S. Schaltegger	2013	Corporate Governance (Bingley)
L.R. Salome, M. van Bottenburg, M. van den Heuvel	2013	Leisure Studies
S. Parra	2013	Journal of Technology Management and Innovation
R. Gupta, A. Pandit, A. Nirjar, P. Gupta	2013	Asian Journal of Management Cases
R. Hallak, G. Assaker	2013	Asia Pacific Journal of Tourism Research
M. Atiq, M. Karatas-Ozkan	2013	International Journal of Entrepreneurship and Innovation
T. Lans, V. Blok, R. Wesselink	2014	Journal of Cleaner Production
B.J. Gray, S. Duncan, J. Kirkwood, S. Walton	2014	Entrepreneurship and Regional Development
K. Fellnhofer, S. Kraus, R.B. Bouncken	2014	International Journal of Business Research
I. Papadopoulos, G. Karagouni, M. Trigkas, Z. Beltsiou	2014	EuroMed Journal of Business
S.J. Willemsen, G. van der Veen	2014	Journal of Place Management and Development
S. Rozenes, I. Kukliansky	2014	International Journal of Information Systems in the Service Sector
K. Djupdal	2014	World Review of Entrepreneurship, Management and Sustainable Development
P. Muñoz, D. Dimov	2015	Journal of Business Venturing
N.M.P. Bocken	2015	Journal of Cleaner Production
J. Pinkse, K. Groot	2015	Entrepreneurship: Theory and Practice
J. Hörisch	2015	Journal of Cleaner Production
E. Kibler, M. Fink, R. Lang, P. Muñoz	2015	Journal of Business Venturing Insights
I. Silajdžić, S. M. Kurtagić, B. Vučijak	2015	Journal of Cleaner Production
K. Djupdal, P. Westhead	2015	International Small Business Journal: Researching Entrepreneurship
K. Schaefer, P.D. Corner, K. Kearins	2015	Organization and Environment
J. Maas, J.F.G. Bunders, M.B.M. Zweekhorst	2015	International Journal of Business and Globalisation

(continued)

Authors	Year	Journal
L. Mayangsari, S. Novani, P. Hermawan	2015	International Journal of Entrepreneurship and Small Business
F. Sáenz-Segura, R.A. Schipper, D. Miranda, J.M. Chaves	2015	Journal on Chain and Network Science
S. Schaltegger, F. Lüdeke-Freund, E.G. Hansen	2016	Organization and Environment
D.E. de Lange	2016	Journal of Cleaner Production
H.C. Hooi, N.H. Ahmad, A. Amran, S.A. Rahman	2016	Management Research Review
N. Yeasmin	2016	Entrepreneurial Business and Economics Review
N. Bank, W. Kanda	2016	Industry and Higher Education
H.J. Steinz, F.J. Van Rijnsoever, F. Nauta	2016	Business Strategy and the Environment
J.-J. Obrecht	2016	International Journal of Entrepreneurship and Small Business
E.-M. Vatamanescu, F. Pinzaru, A.G. Andrei, A. Zbuchea	2016	Transformations in Business and Economics
T.S. Grindsted	2016	Journal of Cleaner Production
R.G. Klapper, V.A. Farber	2016	International Journal of Management Education
C. De Lucia, P. Balena, M.R. Stufano Melone, D. Borri	2016	Journal of Cleaner Production
J.J. Vauterin, T. Virkki-Hatakka	2016	Industry and Higher Education
F.M. Belz, J.K. Binder	2017	Business Strategy and the Environment
W. Stubbs	2017	Business Strategy and the Environment
L. DiVito, R. Bohnsack	2017	Journal of Business Venturing
K.K. Swanson, C. DeVereaux	2017	Annals of Tourism Research
D.E. de Lange	2017	Journal of Cleaner Production
K. Poldner, P. Shrivastava, O. Branzei	2017	Business and Society
P. Muñoz, B. Cohen	2017	Journal of Business Venturing Insights
N. Cherchem	2017	Journal of Family Business Strategy
K. Fellnhofer	2017	Journal of Cleaner Production
F. Gasbarro, E. Annunziata, F. Rizzi, M. Frey	2017	Organization and Environment
J. Klewitz	2017	Innovation
M.A.V. Zacarías, E. Aguiñaga, E.A. Lagunas	2017	International Journal of Trade and Global Markets
K. Poldner, D. Dentoni, O. Ivanova	2017	Journal of Cleaner Production
P. Dickel	2017	Corporate Governance (Bingley)
G. Outsios, S.A. Farooqi	2017	Gender in Management
N.A. Juma, C.D. James, E. Kwesiga	2017	Journal of Small Business and Entrepreneurship
S. Castellano, I. Khelladi, L. Menvielle	2017	International Journal of Entrepreneurship and Small Business

(continued)

Authors	Year	Journal
M. Jayaratne, G.S. Mort, C. D'Souza	2017	Australasian Marketing Journal
V. Vial	2017	Global Business and Organizational Excellence
L. Ploum, V. Blok, T. Lans, O. Omta	2018	Organization and Environment
P. Muñoz, B. Cohen	2018	Business Strategy and the Environment
X. Neumeyer, S.C. Santos	2018	Journal of Cleaner Production
C. Theodoraki, K. Messeghem, M.P. Rice	2018	Small Business Economics
A.M. Vuorio, K. Puumalainen, K. Fellnhofer	2018	International Journal of Entrepreneurial Behaviour and Research
H. Breuer, K. Fichter, F. Lüdeke-Freund, I. Tiemann	2018	International Journal of Entrepreneurial Venturing
K. Fichter, I. Tiemann	2018	Journal of Cleaner Production
R. Hahn, P. Spieth, I. Ince	2018	Journal of Cleaner Production
P. Anbarasan, P. Sushil	2018	Business Strategy and the Environment
S. Schaltegger, M. Beckmann, K. Hockerts	2018	International Journal of Entrepreneurial Venturing
R. Hanohov, L. Baldacchino	2018	International Journal of Entrepreneurial Behaviour and Research
P. Muñoz, G. Cacciotti, B. Cohen	2018	Journal of Business Venturing
D. Fischer, R. Mauer, M. Brettel	2018	International Journal of Entrepreneurial Behaviour and Research
F. Gasbarro, F. Rizzi, M. Frey	2018	International Journal of Entrepreneurial Behaviour and Research
J. Cincera, P. Biberhofer, B. Binka, J. Boman, L. Mindt, M. Rieckmann	2018	Journal of Cleaner Production
P. Muñoz, B. Cohen	2018	Journal of Small Business Management
J. Zeng	2018	International Entrepreneurship and Management Journal
I.A. Davies, L. Chambers	2018	Journal of Cleaner Production
A. Criado-Gomis, M. Iniesta-Bonillo, A. Cervera-Taulet	2018	International Entrepreneurship and Management Journal
S. Ivanova, A. Latyshov	2018	Entrepreneurship and Sustainability Issues
L. Ploum, V. Blok, T. Lans, O. Omta	2018	Journal of Cleaner Production
C.G. Johnsen, L. Olaison, B.M. Sørensen	2018	Organization Studies
E.P. Kiselitsa, N.N. Shilova, I.A. Liman, E.E. Naumenko	2018	Entrepreneurship and Sustainability Issues
P. Muñoz	2018	International Journal of Entrepreneurial Behaviour and Research
J. Hörisch	2018	Journal of Cleaner Production
O. Reynolds, M. Sheehan, R. Hilliard	2018	International Journal of Entrepreneurial Behaviour and Research
A.I. Wahga, R. Blundel, A. Schaefer	2018	International Journal of Entrepreneurial Behaviour and Research

(continued)

Authors	Year	Journal
I. Tiemann, K. Fichter, J. Geier	2018	International Journal of Entrepreneurial Venturing
C. Nhemachena, M. Murimbika	2018	Business Strategy and Development
M. Vlasov, K.J. Bonnedahl, Z. Vincze	2018	Journal of Enterprising Communities
K. Bischoff, C.K. Volkmann	2018	International Journal of Entrepreneurial Venturing
L. Bergset	2018	International Journal of Entrepreneurial Behaviour and Research
B.A. Porter, M.B. Orams, M. Lück	2018	Tourism Planning and Development
J. Chen, L. Chen, J. Chen, K. Xie	2018	Journal of Cleaner Production
I.E. Nikolaou, K. Tasopoulou, K. Tsagarakis	2018	Journal of Entrepreneurship
E. St-Jean, F. Labelle	2018	International Journal of Entrepreneurial Behaviour and Research
B. Mupfasoni, A. Kessler, T. Lans	2018	Journal of Small Business and Enterprise Development
M.R. Ibrahim, A. Shuib, S. Ramachandran, S.H.M. Afandi	2018	International Journal of Business and Society
M.A. Abdullahi, Z. Mohamed, M.N. Shamsudin, J. Sharifuddin, F. Ali	2018	Business Strategy and Development
J.G. York	2018	International Journal of Entrepreneurial Venturing
E. Triantafillidou, S. Tsiaras	2018	Journal for International Business and Entrepreneurship Development
W.R. Meek, D.M. Sullivan	2018	Journal of Developmental Entrepreneurship
N. Richardson	2018	Strategic Change
K. Haviernikivá, M. Kordoš	2019	Entrepreneurship and Sustainability Issues
G. Giudici, M. Guerini, C. Rossi-Lamastra	2019	Small Business Economics
P. Biberhofer, C. Lintner, J. Bernhardt, M. Rieckmann	2019	International Journal of Entrepreneurship and Innovation
S.A. Sunny, C. Shu	2019	Small Business Economics
M. Kant, W. Kanda	2019	Journal of Cleaner Production
S. Testa, K.R. Nielsen, M. Bogers, S. Cincotti	2019	Technological Forecasting and Social Change
B. Hoogendoorn, P. van der Zwan, R. Thurik	2019	Journal of Business Ethics
N. Bento, G. Gianfrate, M.H. Thoni	2019	Journal of Cleaner Production
T. Tarnanidis, J. Papathanasiou, D. Subeniotis	2019	Journal of Business Ethics
A. Nave, M. Franco	2019	Journal of Cleaner Production
M. Wagner, S. Schaltegger, E.G. Hansen, K. Fichter	2019	Small Business Economics
C. Volkmann, K. Fichter, M. Klofsten, D.B. Audretsch	2019	Small Business Economics

(continued)

Authors	Year	Journal
M. Vlasov	2019	Organization and Environment
A.-C. Er, N.F.M. Nawi, M.-Y. Tee, N.I. Ibrahim, N. Bachok	2019	International Journal of Business and Society
Z. Mohamad, A. Nasir	2019	International Journal of Entrepreneurship
D.E. de Lange	2019	Journal of Cleaner Production
A. Kuckertz, E.S.C. Berger, A. Gaudig	2019	Journal of Cleaner Production
T.B. Long, V. Blok, I. Coninx	2019	Journal of Cleaner Production
O. Fatoki	2019	Entrepreneurship and Sustainability Issues
D. de Lange, D. Valliere	2019	Journal of Small Business Management
K. Bischoff	2019	Small Business Economics
S. Pankov, V.K. Velamuri, D. Schneckenberg	2019	Small Business Economics
L. DiVito, Z. Ingen-Housz	2019	Small Business Economics
G. O'Shea, S. Farny, H. Hakala	2019	Small Business Economics
Y. Engel, A. Ramesh, N. Steiner	2019	Journal of Business Venturing
M.P. Johnson, S. Schaltegger	2019	Entrepreneurship: Theory and Practice
M. Ziolo, M. Ben Ghoul	2019	International Journal of Business and Globalisation
M. Franco, M. Rodrigues	2019	Journal of Business Strategy
E. Baraibar-Diez, M.D. Odriozola, E.G. Prieto	2019	International Journal of Entrepreneurship and Innovation Management
S.A. Meshram, A.M. Rawani	2019	International Journal of E-Entrepreneurship and Innovation
E.L. Ramos-Monge, X. Llinàs-Audet, J. Barrena-Martínez	2019	International Journal of Entrepreneurship and Innovation Management
S.B. Soderstrom, K.L. Heinze	2019	Organization and Environment
V. Salmivaara, E. Kibler	2019	Entrepreneurship: Theory and Practice
M. Dressler, I. Paunović	2019	British Food Journal
D. Miragaia, J. Ferreira, A. Carvalho, V. Ratten	2019	Journal of Entrepreneurship and Public Policy
E.B. Villar, F. Miralles	2019	DLSU Business and Economics Review
T. Fatima, A.R. Bilal, M.K. Imran	2019	Emerald Emerging Markets Case Studies
J. Alam, M. Ibn-Boamah, K. Johnson	2019	Strategic Change
J. Faludi, C. Gilbert	2019	Journal of Cleaner Production
P. Udayanan	2019	Entrepreneurial Business and Economics Review

The manufacturer's authorised representative in the EU is Springer Nature Customer Service Centre GmbH, Europaplatz 3, 69115 Heidelberg, Germany. If you have any concerns regarding our products, please contact ProductSafety@springernature.com

Printed and bound by CPI Group (UK) Ltd, Croydon, CR0 4YY
30/09/2026
02225664-0001